# SNORING
## from A to
# ZZZZ

**Snoring From A to ZZZZ** *addresses currently available treatment options for snoring and sleep apnea in an easy-to-understand yet factual, accurate and complete fashion.*

DAVID P. WHITE, M.D., PRESIDENT,
AMERICAN SLEEP DISORDERS ASSOCIATION

*Dr. Lipman has done an admirable job of correlating a gold mine of information on both snoring and sleep apnea. I highly recommend this book as entertaining and informative reading for anyone who has lived with a snorer.*

DAVID B. RUDOLPH, M.D., CLINICAL PROFESSOR,
TUFTS NEW ENGLAND MEDICAL CENTER
BOSTON, MASSACHUSETTS

*At last,* the *definitive book on this all too common and sometimes very serious disorder. Accurate, up-to-date and very readable,* **Snoring From A to ZZZZ** *is a must read for the afflicted and their loved ones.*

DEAN S. EDELL, M.D.
NATIONALLY SYNDICATED RADIO AND TV MEDICAL JOURNALIST

*Snoring is a major barrier to romance. It's hard to be loving and intimate with all that rumbling going on! Dr. Lipman's wonderful book is the perfect prescription for snorers and their partners.* **Snoring From A to ZZZZ** *will help bring snorers from the spare room back into the bedroom . . . and may save millions of marriages!*

GREGORY J.P. GODEK
AUTHOR OF *1001 WAYS TO BE ROMANTIC*

*One of the major dangers of driving—sleepiness behind the wheel—is finally being addressed. The information contained in Dr. Derek Lipman's book* **Snoring From A to ZZZZ** *is of great value to the automobile industry at every level, as well as to every person driving a motor vehicle.*

RON B. TONKIN, PAST PRESIDENT,
NATIONAL AUTOMOBILE DEALER'S ASSOCIATION

# SNORING
## from A to
# ZZZZ
### PROVEN CURES
### FOR THE
### NIGHT'S
### WORST
### NUISANCE

DEREK S. LIPMAN, M.D.

SPENCER PRESS
PORTLAND, OREGON

**SPENCER PRESS**
2525 N.W. LOVEJOY
PORTLAND, OR 97210

Publisher's Cataloging-in-Publication Data
Lipman, Derek, S.
Snoring from a to zzzz: proven cures for the night's worst nuisance/Derek S. Lipman
p.    ill.    cm.
Includes bibliographical references and index.
ISBN  0-9650708-2-4
1. Sleep apnea syndromes—Popular works.
2. Snoring.    I. Title.

RA737. 5 . L57
616.2—dc20        95-72633

Printed in the United States of America

10  9  8  7  6  5  4  3  2

# Disclaimer

This book is intended to provide information and entertainment rather than give specific medical advice or advocate one method of treatment over another.

To accept medical treatment of any kind or undergo surgery is a highly personal decision. That decision should be made only after the treating physician has fully explained every aspect of the recommended therapy or procedure, including the options, risks and potential complications of such treatment.

The author and publisher shall not accept liability or responsibility to any person with respect to loss, injury or damage caused or alleged to be caused by information contained within this book.

In this book, case studies mention certain individuals. Should any of these bear a relationship to a living person, then those characters have no character.

You may return this book to the publisher for a full refund if you do not wish to be bound by the above.

One of my medical school professors was fond of quoting the great physician and teacher, Sir William Osler:

*To study the phenomena of disease without books is to sail an uncharted sea, while to study books without patients it not to go to sea at all.*

I dedicate this book to my patients for taking me along on this voyage of discovery.

In addition, I wish to dedicate this book to my late mother, Constance Ellen Lipman, a former English teacher. She taught me, from an early age, that words are precious things, each with its own special meaning.

# Contents

# Foreword

The sounds of snoring have bothered mankind since the beginning of recorded history, exasperating anyone trying to sleep near a loud snorer. Recently, however, we who snore, and the physicians who treat us, have come to accept snoring as a treatable medical problem, rather than being the butt of numerous tasteless jokes.

Snoring is now recognized as a prominent symptom of sleep apnea, an illness which can disable or cause injury to others. Sleep apnea can be responsible for chronic fatigue, high blood pressure, heart disease, depression, weight gain or impotence. For persons with apnea, such as myself, snoring is no joke. Without diagnosis and treatment, we never get a good night's sleep. As a result, we wake up feeling exhausted, often falling asleep at work, in the midst of social gatherings, or worse, behind the wheels of our cars.

The author has done a great service for those of us with sleep apnea. He explains snoring and sleep apnea with clarity, even whimsy. His book covers every aspect of this problem—recognition of symptoms, diagnosis, testing and treatment options. By making every facet of snoring and sleep apnea crystal clear, Dr. Lipman's book improves the likelihood that we will receive appropriate treatment. As a result, we arrive at a physician's office informed about our choices. We can also give this book to those bothered by our snoring or those who have questions regarding treatment for sleep apnea.

Dr. Derek Lipman has helped snorers far and wide realize that we are persons with an illness, rather than an annoying habit. I heartily recommend *Snoring From A to*

*ZZZZ* as bedtime reading for every snorer and for those
who have to live with one.

Frank T. Adams, Ph.D.
Chairman of the Board of Directors
American Sleep Apnea Association

# Preface

In my 25 years of practice as an ear, nose and throat specialist, I have consulted with many patients and their partners seeking help for their snoring. Sometimes embarrassed, they described, often in extremely colorful terms, how snoring had disrupted their relationships. As a consequence, they were often banished to a spare bedroom in order to get a good night's sleep.

On questioning, many of these snorers admitted to a gradually eroding quality of sleep. Instead of awakening feeling refreshed, they described varying degrees of sleepiness and fatigue during their waking hours. In addition to being disturbed by the snoring, bedroom companions have observed their mate's irregular breathing and apparent choking during the night. Without realizing the full significance, these partners were describing a medical condition which we now call *sleep apnea*.

Until the early 1980's, however, there was little help available for a snorer beyond fitting their partner with ear plugs. For a physician, it was as frustrating for me to turn patients away as it was for them to leave without obtaining any kind of comfort or relief.

Around that time, reports of improved techniques in the diagnosis and treatment of snoring and sleep-induced breathing disorders began to appear in the medical literature. Becoming intrigued by this emerging subject, I attended courses and symposia, visiting sleep disorders clinics, learning these techniques from the physicians who had pioneered them.

In addition to accumulating information about snoring from the medical literature, my interest led me to popular magazine articles on this subject, going back to the turn of the century, containing delightful anecdotes about snoring and snorers. In the dusty pages of a 1926 *Ladies' Home Journal,* I discovered the following plea:

> **Experts are sending us mixed messages about snoring. One thing is for certain, there is no simple answer. If you have a solution, write a book. It can't miss. The world is still waiting. . . and snoring.**

Here is that book.

*Snoring From A to ZZZZ* was never intended as a medical text or comprehensive review of sleep-related breathing disorders. Rather, this book was conceived for snorers and their frustrated partners, aptly called "snorees". It was written to entertain, educate and encourage them to no longer take their problem lying down!

It is my intention to show snorers *and* snorees that snoring can be far more than bedroom sound-effects. It may, in many cases, be the cardinal symptom of a potentially serious underlying medical condition. By regarding snoring as a legitimate medical complaint rather than an annoying personal habit, I wish to alert primary care physicians to myriad problems which may occur when we close our eyes at night and switch over to automatic pilot.

These introductory words were written in 1989, when my first manuscript for a book on snoring was accepted for publication by a sympathetic editor, who somehow saw this book as a salvation for her marriage. At that time, she was married to the snoring champion of Pennsylvania!

*Stop Your Husband From Snoring* was published by Rodale Press the following year, well received in the United States and being translated into German and Italian editions.

Since publication of that book, however, we have seen a rising tide of activity in the field of sleep disorders. A National Commission on Sleep Disorders Research was mandated by Congress; a separate Department of Sleep Disorders was recently established by the National Institutes of Health. As more physicians dedicate their professional activities to the clinical or research aspects of sleep, increasing numbers of valuable publications on these subjects appear in the medical literature.

Sleep disorders clinics continue to be established throughout the United States and, in fact, throughout the world. Unattended sleep studies have achieved new levels of accuracy and sophistication. The range of available medical and surgical treatments for snoring and sleep apnea continues to expand. Introduction of the medical laser now allows surgeons to offer safe and effective office treatment. Additionally, the recent high-tech application of radiofrequency tissue volume reduction and coblation have ushered in a new era of safe and successful snoring therapies.

I sincerely hope that this book will serve as a source of useful information to snorers and their families, as well as providing both primary care physicians and specialists with a handy guide to a group of frequently encountered medical conditions, together with some solutions for curing the night's worst nuisance.

It is my wish that this information will help many of you, among the millions of snorers, to obtain relief, enjoy the vitalizing benefits of a good night's sleep, bringing your long-suffering partners out of the spare room . . . and back into the bedroom.

Derek S. Lipman, M.D.<br>Lake Oswego, Oregon

# Acknowledgments

I am deeply grateful to many people who were so generous with their time and talent while working on this book.

David Morgan, my agent and friend, believed in this project when it was a mere twinkle in my eye. Editors at Rodale Press, Sharon Faelten and Charles Gerras. Bernard Kurman, foreign rights agent, has introduced translations of my book in many countries throughout the world. F. Blair Simmons, M.D., Division of Otolaryngology-Head and Neck Surgery, Stanford University Medical Center, taught me the principles of surgery for sleep apnea; Regina P. Walker, M.D. and Yosef P. Krespi, M.D., leaders in laser surgery, graciously shared information and illustrations; Nikhil J. Bhatt, M.D., pioneer laser surgeon, whose contributions have yet to be recognized; Joel G. Cohen, M.D., F.A.C.S.; Frank T. Adams, Ph.D., chairman of the board, American Sleep Apnea Association.

Sleep disorders specialists Louis S. Libby, M.D., Gerald B. Rich, M.D., Keith L. Ironside Jr., M.D., and John J. Greve, M.D., provided information and inspiration; Laurence I. Barsh, D.M.D., my friend and fellow board member, American Sleep Apnea Association; members of the administrative staff, American Sleep Disorders Association; instructors of the American Academy of Otolaryngology-Head and Neck Surgery, whose superb presentations and informal discussions provided so much valuable information. Lionel M. Nelson, M.D., medical director, Somnus, always willing to share information and experience.

Librarians at Multnomah County Library, Lake Oswego Library, Legacy Emanuel Hospital and Providence St. Vincent Hospital medical libraries; medical photographers Connie Hough and Morgan Lavin.

Allen D. Davey, director of the British Snoring and Sleep

Apnoea Association, whose tireless efforts have done so much to educate the public in the United Kingdom.

Operating room personnel and nursing staff, Legacy Emanuel Hospital, Portland; members of the Department of Anesthesia at Emanuel have provided support and safety for my patients over many years.

Talented medical artists, Joan Livermore, C.M.I. and Geoffrey Sauncy helped bring this book to life; Laurie Tolmasoff-Collins, speedy and accurate transcriptionist, with the patience of Job.

Susan Talmadge, a bibliophile with impeccable taste, helped edit my manuscript, gently yet firmly applying her blue pencil to the saga of Ozzie the snoring owl.

Peter Harris, ESC Laser Systems, always ready with new ideas, instruments and information; and Roger J. Porter, Professor of English, Reed College, Portland.

My loyal and hard-working office staff, Marlowe Hopper and Bernetta Johnson. Kathy Hanlon Stacy, who has administered my busy practice for so many years with elegance, charm and metronomic efficiency.

Finally, I must pay tribute to my wonderful family. My wife Lydia has staunchly supported me through thick and thin; my daughter Nicole, a recent graduate of Harvard Law School and my son Grant, a medical student, while a constant source of pride and inspiration, have jointly voiced their genuine concern that any reputable company would seriously consider publishing their father's particular brand of humor.

Authors of nonfiction books such as this are not encouraged to talk about themselves. Without showing my readers the family photo albums, I must confess that although this project consumed many hundreds of long hours, sometimes after gruelling days in the office or operating room, I have thoroughly enjoyed every moment of the experience.

# SNORING
## from A to
# ZZZZ

# Chapter 1

# Is There a Snorer in the House?

## Snoring Stories: Some Short, Some Tall

S leep.
Poets have praised it as the ultimate symbol for rest and quietude. Longfellow referred to it as "night's repose," Shakespeare called it "nature's soft nurse," and Keats exulted "O magic sleep! O comfortable bird/That broodest o'er the troubled sea of the mind/Till it is hushed and smooth."

But few of us are poets, and for many, sleep is far from "magic" and often quite far from "hushed and smooth." As an anxious wife wrote to a popular newspaper columnist:

> I am desperately trying to find a cure for my husband's snoring. After being married for 27 years, I am convinced that there is no cure other than killing him, which is illegal, as you know.

Snoring has been with us since the beginning of time. It is not difficult to imagine our prehistoric ancestors sleeping in their caves, rumbling and snorting in the flickering fire light. In fact, according to one theory, present-day snorers are simply reenacting the primitive instinct of making ferocious noises at night to protect their sleeping womenfolk by keeping dangerous animals at bay. Many men may cite this theory as proof of their manly devotion, saying "I'm just keeping the woolly mammoths away from you, Dear." But few women today seem willing to buy it!

*More than 40 million Americans snore.* For some, snoring is no more than an occasional and innocuous habit. But for countless bedroom companions it represents an unending nightly disturbance, turning what Milton called the "kindly dew of sleep" into a disruptive, nerve-wracking experience. No doubt this is what philosopher/

author Anthony Burgess had in mind when he wrote his famous epigram: "Laugh and the world laughs with you; snore and you sleep alone."

## Snorers Are Immune to the Noise

Regarded as everything from a bother to a joke, the snorer has been looked upon as a whimsical oddity—a kind of misfit whose trumpetings make him an ideal subject for humorists. Mark Twain devoted an entire essay to the subject, marveling that the snorer could somehow manage to sleep blissfully, while those around him had to cover their ears. "There ain't no way to find out," he moaned, "why a snorer can't hear himself snore.". And later, Twain's immortal Huckleberry Finn said of his father in awe: "Pap used to sleep . . . with the hogs, but Laws bless you, he just lifts things when he snores."

Some might say that America was settled as the round-about result of a snore. John Smith, a young English commander in charge of a 150-horse cavalry unit (assigned to drive the Turks from Hungary), found his way to Pocahontas and into American history because of a sentry who slept, snoring at his post. Drawn by the sound of the sentry's extraordinary sawing, a passing army of Tartars discovered Smith's sleeping camp and attacked immediately. In the massacre that followed, Smith was captured and sold as a slave in Constantinople. He escaped and walked hundreds of miles across Europe, finally arriving back in England. There, using new maps and data gathered as he worked his way home, he organized an expedition for the New World land of Virginia. Good fortune led him to befriend Pocahontas, the Indian chief's daughter, who saved him from beheading. And the rest, as they say, is history. . .

Even in the military, where all things male are celebrated, robust snoring is neither envied nor aspired to. The illustrious Roman statesman, Marcus Cato withered one of his generals by declaring, "His snore is louder than his battle cry."

Perhaps the most celebrated snorer to wear the uniform of his country was Private Tony Rodriguez, a United States M.P. stationed in London, England, during World War II. A barracks' mate, who evidently suffered through many a sleepless night, finally wrote these program notes about Tony's virtuoso performance:

> The first movement is pastoral. Then . . . the violas and double basses enter vigorously. The second movement introduces the sounds of war. Fighter planes rise in a screeching spiral to give battle to a bomber formation. The intermingled aircraft fire all their guns and cannons, and the bombers release heavy salvos of high-explosive bombs.

Tony shifts in his sleep, and the third movement begins, more soul-searing than the second. A man is drowning in a heavy storm at sea. We hear the mountainous crash of the waves, the screams of the lost man, the mournful bellows of a whistling buoy and the peals of angry thunder. Then comes the unbearable crash of the massed kettledrums. A shoe hits Tony. The symphony is over.

The records show that Rodriguez's commanding officer saved the morale of the company by ordering a special hut built for him. Presumably Tony continued to develop his musical gifts while sleeping alone.

Snoring respects neither social nor economic barriers. Numerous presidents of the United States are said to have been impressive snorers, including Washington, Lincoln, both Adamses, VanBuren, Fillmore, Pierce, Buchanan,

Grant, Hays, Cleveland, McKinley, Taft, Harding and Franklin Delano Roosevelt. Despite this impressive bi-partisan roll call of stentorian snorers among our leaders, it is comforting to know that there has never been a divorce in the White House.

The British ex-Prime Minister, Sir Winston Churchill, was an inveterate snorer, according to a naval officer who had the misfortune of sharing a cabin with him aboard a battleship. And, although it sullies their images to some extent, those fabled ladies' men, Beau Brummell and Mussolini, were known among their female admirers as prodigious snorers.

## Duel of the Decibels

Some of the truly outrageous snorers managed to capitalize on their vice. David Bishop, reputed to be the champion snorer of the great state of Arizona, was challenged by Texan Steve Hawkins to a Snore-Down. The bet was $10,000. The two men checked into adjoining rooms at a local hotel to do their stuff for the judges (the town undertaker and a magistrate), who stood outside the bedroom doors to evaluate the thunder. But the contest was declared a draw.

A second bout was scheduled, but before it began, the judges were approached by a white-haired old man, a stranger in town, who wore ill-fitting clothes and spoke with a heavy German accent. He introduced himself as the famous Professor August von Dusenberg, inventor of the phonometer, a scientific sound-measuring machine. The professor volunteered the use of his invention as a foolproof way to decide the winner. His offer was gratefully accepted.

When the snoring began that evening, the professor

pressed the button to start his machine. Fascinated, the judges watched as a series of staccato snorts advanced the indicator closer and closer to the highest mark. Suddenly, there was a mighty roar of a snore and something snapped in the machine. The indicator shot back to zero and stayed there. And that's where the story ends. Bishop's and Hawkins' snoring had broken the machine! No clear winner ever emerged in that contest. Nor was a stronger phonometer ever invented.

The true snoring champion of the world is Melvin Switzer, according to the *Guinness Book of World Records.* Using recording equipment provided by the local Noise Abatement Society, mighty Mel outblasted his competitors during the early morning hours in a contest held at Hever Castle in Kent, England on June 28, 1984. He proudly took first place with a snore score of 87.5 decibels—the equivalent of a motorcycle revving up at close quarters. For the record, Switzer's wife is deaf in one ear.

But Mel was merely warming up his pipes. Eight years later, at the South View Hotel in Lyndhurst, England he outsnored all challengers. On the evening of October 29, 1992, Mr. Switzer successfully defended his title with an ear-shattering 92 decibel victory.

Needless to say, hotel guests in Lyndhurst that night regarded sleep as something of an impossible dream. . .

## The Night's Worst Nuisance

It's no surprise then that snoring has turned roommates into enemies, cut short the budding relationship of many a young couple and blasted the bliss out of the honeymoon for numerous newlyweds. Once married, the language wives use to report on their husband's snoring is alternately anguished, desperate, bitter, resigned or wist-

**Snoring Champion of the World**

ful. This letter represents many that distressed and exhausted wives write to newspaper columnists, suggesting that snoring may rank with infidelity as a prime cause of marital discord:

I woke up at three o'clock this morning, wondering who was mowing our lawn. Another time, I dreamed a tugboat was stuck in our bedroom, frantically signaling for help. This has been going on for 15 years. I can't remember the last time I had a good night's sleep. When I threaten to go to another bedroom, my husband says he didn't marry me to sleep alone. I have begged him to see a doctor or try remedies I have heard about. But he won't. He says I snore. Can you help me?

*Frantic In Fresno*

More than 150,000 replies poured in. Some readers offered sympathy; others advice. More than 90 percent described moving to another bedroom as soon as one became available.

Sprinkled with wisdom and imagination, their letters portrayed wives whom fate had somehow left with the choice of either lying awake in the darkness while the walls around them shook, or taking a lonely trip down the hall to the spare bedroom. Their marriages, once the stuff of dreams, had turned into nightmares.

## Things That Go ZZZZ in the Night

Snoring can also cause misery in the great outdoors. On a hunting trip to Africa, two close friends pitched their tents and settled down for the night, after being cautioned by their guides to keep loaded rifles by their sides as a safeguard against marauding animals. Awakened by the sounds of snarling, grunting and roaring, one of the hunters reached for his rifle, firing bullets wildly into the darkness. The awakened guides carefully searched the entire camp with flashlights, discovering no trace of any wild beast. The "animal" sounds, of course, came from the other hunter's tent. . .

A fire fighter, sleeping in his station dormitory, awoke to the sound of the fire-truck revving up. Pulling on his clothes in a blind panic, fearful that the truck would leave without him, he rushed into the station garage where all was silent. Returning to the dormitory, he discovered the source of the noise. It was one of his colleagues, whose snoring matched the volume of a fire-rig in high gear.

## Snoring Through the Flooring

An understandably concerned California citizen recently wrote this letter to a well-known syndicated newspaper columnist:

> "What is the world coming to when a person can be arrested and fined for snoring? A college student who lives in Davis, California, called the police to complain about his neighbor making so much noise that he couldn't sleep. The police arrived, expecting to encounter a wild party, but to their surprise, found a sleeping woman, snoring very loudly. The 30-year-

old mother of two was given a ticket for disturbing the peace, together with a $135.00 fine. Incensed, she hired a lawyer to sue the city for making her an object of ridicule as well as damaging her health. She claims that she is now unable to sleep for fear the police will give her another summons. Isn't this outrageous?"

Here's the reply:

"Fining the woman *was* outrageous. I do hope, however, that she will have a simple surgical procedure to correct the problem. The $135.00 fine should be returned!"

A San Francisco woman claimed that in 35 years of marriage she had never shared a bedroom with her husband because of his infernal snoring. However, she slept like a log during the recent earthquake (measuring 6.9 on the Richter scale) while the house collapsed around her.

## The Trouble with George

Perhaps the most celebrated letter about snoring in matrimony came not from a woman but from a man. In April 1915, George Little of Pittsburgh, Pennsylvania, wrote to the *Ladies' Home Journal* asking readers for advice on how to stop his disruptive habit. Readers' replies poured in from all over the country with recommendations, information and sympathy. So numerous were the responses that the *Journal* started a column which ran for a year, entitled, "How Can George Stop Snoring?" These were among the answers that came in:

> I never used to snore until my hair began to fall out, and the balder I got the louder I snored . . . Finally

my wife . . . brought from town one day a slumber cap, which I have worn ever since—at night, of course—and I have ceased to snore. You see, my hair was so thin that I caught cold every night, and stuffing up, would snore.

Signed: *Atlanta*

Do you realize that Indians never snore? I have slept many a night in their teepees and never heard a sound. The secret of it is that Indian children are always taught to sleep with their mouth closed so as to prevent throat troubles. Here is a hint for mothers if we are to prevent another generation of snorers.

Signed: *Mrs. D.R.*

As snoring comes from within, we must look for the cause within. If a man were truly unselfish and refined, he would not snore. He would be the same within as without and the same asleep as awake. What we are within is bound to come out. Therefore, the only permanent cure for snoring is to be wholly unselfish in every thought, and natural refinement will come; and then—men will not snore.

Signed: *Helen Howard*

Eventually, this unending flood of letters from thousands of anxious readers forced the editors of the *Journal* to cry, "Enough! If Mr. Little hasn't enough 'cures' by this time, the *Journal* fears he is hopeless!"

Too bad George didn't see this ad running in the newspapers of the day:

I Can Absolutely Cure Snoring

By a simple remedy that all physicians will unqualifiedly endorse. No medication, no

mechanical contrivances; just a simple rule, which
followed, does away with even the most aggravated
cases of snoring.
   *Send $1 to* _____

Understandably excited, many snorers immediately sent
in their money and just as quickly received a card with this
printed response:

An Absolute Cure
for Snoring
**Don't Go to Sleep**

While such stories showed that snoring could bring out
the larceny in us, other accounts indicate that snoring gave
rise to even more drastic "cures." For example, in
Budapest, in 1923, a woman was arrested for murder when
she admitted that she could no longer tolerate her
husband's snoring, finally pulling out a pistol and killing
him. And as recently as 1989, in Winthrop, Massachusetts, a man stood trial for allegedly strangling his elderly
hospital roommate because the victim's snoring kept him
awake all night.

Before saying, "I do", perhaps every bride-to-be should switch a noise-level meter on her future mate. However, mere snoring without any other provocation does *not* constitute legal grounds for divorce, according to the Honorable Judge Samuel H. Gilbert of Cuyahoga County Court in Cleveland, Ohio.

In southeastern Oklahoma, a man sued for divorce because his wife snored. The husband, however, was forced to drop his lawsuit when he learned that her stertorous breathing was a psychosomatic condition, traceable to early childhood when she was frightened by a noisy oil pump, operating at close range. Next case, please . . .

John Wesley Hardin, the fabled gunfighter, became incensed by the snoring of a man in the room next to his at the American House Hotel in Abilene, Texas. Not one to waste time with his feelings, Hardin began firing his gun through the bedroom wall. The first bullet awoke the stranger; the second one killed him. Years later, Hardin tried to set the record straight. "They tell lots of lies about me," he complained. "They say I killed six or seven men for snoring. Well, it ain't true; I only killed one."

Regardless of the number, Hardin certainly diminished the population of snorers in Texas. But he left plenty behind. However, nobody knows exactly how many serious snorers shake the shutters every night.

## Snorers: Wake Up and Be Counted!

Virtually all of us snore now and then. Much of it is mild or occasional snoring—as when a man comes home after a tiring day, falls asleep after dinner, and begins to saw away. Given a poke in the ribs, he changes position, and his snoring stops.

Generally, researchers don't include this type of snoring in any statistical study. Additionally, even truly committed snorers do not readily admit to their habit—so studies of its prevalence are all the more difficult and imprecise. In fact, it wasn't until 1968 when Marcus Boulware, Ph.D., a speech language pathologist, director of the Speech and Hearing Program at Florida A.& M. University in Tallahassee, and a pioneer snore therapist as well, made a significant attempt to research the incidence of snoring. Upon questioning 50 state health departments for information on snoring statistics, he found that there were none. A man whose snoring had nearly ended his own marriage, Dr. Boulware asked for and received a $100,000 research grant from the National Institutes of Health to find a cure for snoring. His initiative, known as the *Sonorous Breathing Research Project*, must have inspired other researchers throughout the world to delve into the mysteries of snoring.

---

### Silent Night

"It blasts the silence of the night like an open-throttled Mack truck warming into an uphill climb. It crashes through the central nervous system like a jackhammer; it whines like a chain saw wasting a forest. It is punctuated by uneven arrhythmic snorts—the triumphant blurt of water buffalo."

Marcia Cohen, *Ladies' Home Journal*, October 1976.
© Copyright 1976 Meredith Corporation.

---

In 1978, a team of medical researchers led by Elio Lugaresi, M.D., conducted a study among the inhabitants of San Marino, an independent republic of 20,000 people in northern Italy. From a questionnaire on snoring and sleep disturbances, Dr. Lugaresi determined that 20 percent of all the respondents snored regularly; that twice as many males as females admitted to snoring; and that snoring in men and women appeared to increase with age. Between the ages of 30 and 35, 20 percent of males and 5 percent of females snored regularly. From ages 60 to 65, however, 60 percent of the men reported snoring and so did 40 percent of the women.

In a 1983 investigation done in Toronto on the prevalence of snoring, questionnaires were given to 254 consecutive patients attending a family practice clinic in the city and 25 consecutive patients in a rural community clinic in northern Ontario. Despite the environmental and geographic differences, results in each group were so similar that they were not separated in the analysis.

- ♦ 86 percent of the women said their husbands snored.
- ♦ 52 percent of the women said they were troubled by their husbands' snoring.
- ♦ 57 percent of the men said their wives snored.
- ♦ 15 percent of the men said that they were troubled by their wives' snoring.
- ♦ The majority of snorers were male, outnumbering the females ten to one.

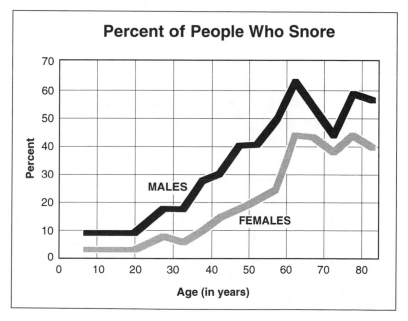

But helpful as these findings are, more studies must be conducted before we can get an accurate idea about the universality of this habit. In the meantime, the expanding number of sleep disorders centers and medical awareness of sleep-related breathing conditions are contributing to a deeper, more sophisticated body of literature on the subject.

## Some *Good* Snoring Stories

Before we explore these findings, let's return to our history of snoring to demonstrate that snoring does indeed have a *positive* side.

Bert Bacharach, a journalist for the *Indianapolis Star*, wrote an article in 1967, describing how snoring refreshes our blood when its oxygen content falls during sleep. Along the same supposedly healthy lines, Dr. Hoppe, a German physician, theorized as far back as 1841, that snoring is a necessary function for clearing mucus from our throat walls.

Ormund Powers could have been the first columnist to suggest that snoring may be a source of comfort and reassurance. "Snoring is the magic of sleep" he wrote in the *Orlando Sentinel-Star*. "It causes far less difficulties among married couples than the absence of snoring brought about when the snorer is not there." Echoing this sentiment was a letter to columnist Abigail Van Buren from a widow, lamenting that to her, snoring would be the sweetest sound this side of heaven. Perhaps it was such sentiments that led to immortalizing the charm of the snore by naming an inn I came across near Victoria, British Columbia: Great-Snoring-On-Sea.

And finally, this delightful short story "The Snoring Beauty", by Anne Douglas Sedgwick, published many years ago in *Harper's Magazine:*

Launcelot Mainwaring was clearly falling head over heels for a beautiful young lady, Elizabeth Thayer, while vacationing in Paris, where they were both staying in the same hotel near the Champs Elysees.

After being introduced by mutual friends, Mainwaring invited Ms. Thayer to attend a performance of the opera with him. By the end of the second act, he was hopelessly in love with her.

Returning to the hotel, they retired to their adjacent rooms, whereupon Mainwaring was suddenly awakened by the deafening sound of snoring coming from the room where his loved one slept.

After enduring three nights of this fearsome din, Mainwaring took his beloved aside, confessed his undying love, and, with unabashed candor, told of his concern about her terrible snoring. Elizabeth, upon hearing this, dropped into a nearby chair, shaking with laughter. Finally controlling herself, she revealed that the source of the snoring was her little dog Toto. "But," she added, "you are a perfect hero. How you must have suffered these nights. I think," she said, her eyes aglow with passion for her new suitor, "you are a man to be adored."

## A Brighter Future

Those who have attempted to go beyond folk remedies and seek professional help have followed further on the path of frustration. Until recently, the medical profession was sadly lacking in a scientific approach to this subject, and had little in the way of remedies to offer any snoring patient.

As recently as 20 years ago, for example, the grim prognosis for snorers was summed up by the editor of the British Medical Association's popular monthly journal *Family Doctor*: "I'm not hopeful about a cure for snoring," he wrote. "It is unlikely that anyone will come up with anything dramatic or sensational."

Today, however, snoring has graduated from being regarded as a hopeless nightly nuisance to the status of a legitimate medical problem—as respectable a symptom as back pain or headache. Researchers and clinicians with an interest in sleep disorders have finally isolated the underlying causes of snoring while uncovering a variety of closely associated medical conditions. They have now established realistic treatments which can bring gratifying results to both snorers and snorees.

# The Great International Noise Neutralizer

Even in Bavaria, snoring is not exactly *The Sound of Music*. So be prepared to declare peace wherever you travel. Here's how to be sure you're understood when you want to curb that bedlam in the boudoir:

Relax in Rome, rage:
*"Impedisci a tuo marito di  russare!"*

Pass a pleasant night in Paris, plead:
*"Empêcher votre mari de ronfler!"*

Ease the pain in Spain, complain:
*"¡No dejes que tu marido ronque!"*

Cut the cacophony in Copenhagen, command:
*"Stop din mands snorken!"*

Head off a Hungarian rhapsody, rasp:
*"Hogyan érjük el, hogy féjünk ne horkoljon!"*

Get some ZZZZ in Zambia, say:
*"Lesha minkonono ya mulume woobe!"*

# Chapter 2

# Things That Go ZZZZ in the Night:

## Searching for the Cause

I n the first chapter we looked at snoring in the superfi-
cial way people usually do—as a stressful nuisance—
funny to some and infuriating to others. But to understand it fully, we need to know what the term *snoring*
really means. Unfortunately, it's easier to discover the
causes of snoring than to define it.

Snoring has been called "the night's worst nuisance"
and has also been referred to, albeit somewhat indelicately,
as "the world's second most anti-social noise."

*Webster's New International Dictionary* defines snoring as "breathing during sleep with a rough, hoarse noise
due to vibration of the uvula and soft palate." However,
most ear, nose and throat specialists now subscribe to the
definition that snoring is "any resonant noise produced in
the upper respiratory tract during sleep." This working
definition was agreed upon in a survey conducted by Dr.
Marcus Boulware in 1968 among a hundred ear, nose

and throat physicians practicing in Europe, Canada, England and the United States. But the descriptions of that "resonant noise" vary widely, from snorting, rasping, choking and gasping to rattling, sawing, rumbling and hissing.

Obviously, we can describe snoring in myriad ways, just as Eskimos have a hundred different words for snow, and each is correct, depending on our individual experience. Perhaps Mark Twain put it best when he wrote that snoring is simply "sleeping out loud."

## What's Your Snore Level?

To obtain a more precise frame of reference, physicians have developed an objective classification system for the amount of noise produced by snoring.

**Mild Snoring:** Occasional snoring, usually while the sleeper is lying on his back and is overtired or has drunk too much alcohol or eaten too much.

**Moderate Snoring:** Frequent snoring, occurring in all body positions.

**Severe Snoring:** Very loud snoring throughout the night in all body positions, heard from one or two rooms away.

**Heroic Snoring:** Extremely loud snoring, heard from three to four rooms away or throughout the entire house.

Snorers graduating with such honors are sometimes known as *Stentorian* snorers. Their title is deservedly in tribute to Stentor, a legendary Roman herald, possessing a voice which equalled the volume of fifty ordinary men.

Depending on the hearing acuity and tolerance of the snoree, one reasonably reliable method of assessing any snorer's damage control is to estimate the distance from

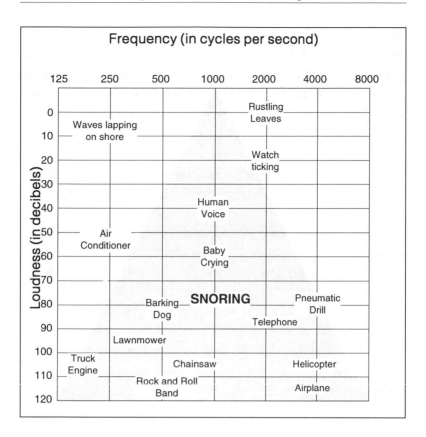

which he or she can be heard. Hence, one-room, two-room, three-room and even across-the-street snorers. Enough to make a social pariah of any snorer, this appraisal has led to any number of colorfully descriptive terms, including "major league snoring" and "baritone saxophone snoring". Judgment solely by volume, therefore, could ultimately result in the cruel yet candid, "one-more-night-of-this-and-I-am-filing-for-divorce snoring!"

Though far from exact, these descriptions do allow us to explore the causes of snoring by associating it with two distinct facts: First, snoring occurs only during sleep; and second, the sounds of snoring are produced in the air passages of the nose and throat, which we refer to as the *upper respiratory tract.*

## Some Puzzles of Snoring

Everyone knows that snoring occurs during sleep. But the questions that have always mystified the partners of snorers and, until recently, physicians as well, are these: Why does snoring occur *only* during sleep? And why are we more likely to snore when we sleep on our back than on our stomach? Why, in other words, don't we snore standing up? Or when we're awake?

Scientific research into sleep didn't begin until late in the nineteenth century, when the electrical activity of the brains of rabbits, cats and monkeys was recorded. Then, many years later, in 1929, a German psychiatrist, Hans Berger, M.D., recorded human electrical brain activity, coining the term *electroencephalogram* (EEG) for this process. His work prepared the way for examining various brain functions—normal activities such as sleep, as well as numerous disorders of the brain and nervous system.

But Dr. Berger's findings about electrical activity of the brain during sleep were virtually ignored for nearly a decade. Then, in 1937, a team of independent researchers confirmed and advanced his findings through their all-night sleep studies, which demonstrated alternating stages of sleep, distinguished by the brain's varying electrical patterns during each stage.

In 1952, researchers at the University of Chicago discovered the *rapid eye movement* (REM) stage of sleep, named for the rapid eye movements associated with it. Dr. Nathaniel Kleitman, a professor of physiology, who at that time was the only person in the world devoting his entire career to the study of sleep, together with Eugene Aserinsky, a graduate student, documented eye movement activity during sleep. This pair of innovative scientists recorded electrical signals generated by eyeball movements. Presumably, REM sleep eluded earlier researchers because it looked so much like an awake period when recorded on

# Riding the Sleep-Wake Cycle

We know that sleep provides restoration for our body as well as our mind. And all living creatures have cycles of alternating activity and rest. For some animals, this cycle is determined by environmental changes such as fluctuation of the tides; for others, a change in seasons may signal the switch from activity to hibernation. In man, the sleep-wake cycle occurs over a period of approximately 24 hours (25 hours to be exact), apparently governed by an internal clock as well as outside changes such as darkness or light. This pattern, called *circadian* (around the day) rhythm, is established in infants after three or four months and continues throughout life.

Does our internal clock run down with age? No one knows. But age does seem to reset it. The elderly tend to go to bed earlier than young people, wake up earlier, and generally need shorter total sleep time.

Lack of sleep or sudden changes in the sleep-wake cycle can, and does, produce alterations in mood, performance and vigilance. These disturbances can vary in severity, depending upon the number of hours shifted, the frequency of the work shifts, and the amount of time allowed for new normal sleep-wake cycles to develop. Similar sleep disturbances are experienced by air travelers, whose jet lag is a result of disrupted body-rhythms due to changing time zones.

an EEG printout. These researchers thought that their subjects had simply awakened during the night, when, in fact (and this was the most exciting understanding to come from the discovery of REM sleep), they were *dreaming*.

When sleeping subjects were awakened during bursts

of rapid eye movement, they immediately recalled vivid dreams; when no eye movements were present, they rarely remembered any dreaming.

This breakthrough in the mysterious phenomenon we know as dreaming, set the stage for research into a host of medical conditions affecting us only during sleep. Additional eye movement studies were published in 1957 by Dr. William Dement, a disciple of Dr. Kleitman. Although his paper received little notice at the time of publication, it ultimately became one of the most-cited scientific papers of all time.

## Matched, Hatched...and Dispatched

ON THIS BED WE ARE CONCEIVED, WE ARE BORN, WE DIE, AND WE SPEND FULLY A THIRD OF OUR LIVES

**A statue in Rome, Italy dedicated to a bed.**

# We Sleep in Stages

Today, we recognize that sleep passes through two distinct phases: *REM sleep* and *non-REM sleep* (NREM). A closer look at REM and NREM sleep brings us to our first answer concerning questions about the causes of snoring and its curious association with sleep.

**Stage 1—NREM sleep:** A transitional stage between wakefulness and sleep, usually lasting 5 to 10 minutes. Breathing becomes slow and regular, the heart rate decreases and we see slow, rolling eye movements. This stage accounts for 5 to 10 percent of a person's total sleep time.

**Stage 2—NREM sleep:** A deeper stage of sleep, where fragmented thoughts and images pass through the mind. Eye movements usually disappear, muscles relax and there is very little body movement. This stage predominates in adults, representing about 50 percent of total sleep time.

**Stage 3—NREM sleep:** Further deepening of sleep with additional slowing of heart and breathing rates. The body's temperature falls; eye movements are absent. This phase comprises approximately 25 percent of the total sleep time in children and adolescents, declines slightly in young adults and decreases dramatically in middle age and older years.

**Stage 4—NREM sleep:** The deepest phase of sleep. Arousal in this stage is the most difficult. Typically, sleepwalking and bed-wetting occur at this time. Stage 4 sleep usually occurs only during the first third of the night, after which NREM sleep does not progress beyond stage 3. Because these two phases of sleep are so similar, researchers have frequently described them in combination. Together they comprise 10 to 20 percent of our total sleep time, diminishing with age.

The NREM stages of our sleep cycle are notable for their physiological rest and quiet. Eye movements are infrequent, heart and respiratory rates are reduced and the body is still. When awakened from NREM sleep, people commonly describe vague fragmented thoughts, scenes or images.

**Stage of REM sleep:** After about 90 minutes of NREM sleep, the first period of REM sleep begins. Initially lasting a few minutes, the REM phase increases to 15 or 20 minutes' duration as sleep progresses.

This phase is distinguished from other sleep stages by a dramatic decrease in muscle tone. The skeletal muscles of the neck, arms and legs are essentially paralyzed. Breathing becomes irregular, the heart rate increases and the eyes display rapid, darting movements. The soft tissues of the upper airway, including the tongue, soft palate and uvula, are completely relaxed. During this phase, the brain's oxygen consumption increases. Sweating, shivering and other body temperature-regulatory mechanisms are usually absent during REM sleep.

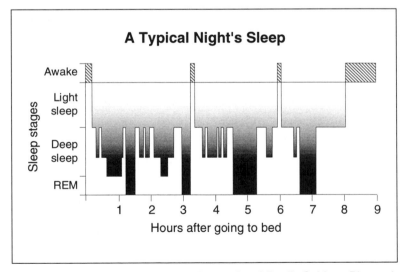

From *Snoring and Sleeping Apnea: Personal and Family Guide to Diagnosis and Treatment*, by Ralph A. Pascualy, M.D. and Sally Warren Soest, M.S., published by Demos Vermande, 1995.

## A Busy Time for Your Brain

REM sleep is the sleep stage of dreaming, typified by vivid, active dreams, consisting of complex symbols and images. Over 70 percent of adults awakened during REM sleep report dreaming. This stage constitutes about 20 percent of the total sleep time for an adult.

The cycle of sleep stages continues throughout the night as we alternate between NREM and REM sleep. Most commonly, the NREM stages develop during the first third of the sleep period; REM sleep and stage 2 NREM sleep predominate during the last third. REM sleep usually enters the cycle as we move from stage 3 or 4 NREM sleep back to stage 2; the whole cycle repeats itself in time periods ranging from 70 to 120 minutes. As you would expect, those who require a greater amount of sleep spend more time in REM sleep, but even whose who require very little sleep go through this customary cycle.

Theories abound as to how and why we use REM sleep and its associated dream state to reenact and process experiences we have had during wakefulness. Under ideal conditions of sleep, our bodies are virtually at rest, therefore permitting the greatest attention to mental (psychological) activity. But studies also show that REM sleep occurs in unborn babies. Obviously, more research must be conducted before we can grasp the full meaning and value of REM sleep.

Before we examine the mechanisms and causes of snoring, it is useful to focus in some detail on the phenomenon of dreaming, because, as you will learn in subsequent chapters, the dream state has a very close relationship to some medical conditions called *sleep-induced breathing disorders*, in all of which snoring is a cardinal feature.

# Dreams: Movies of the Mind

A dream is essentially an hallucination—usually visual, but occasionally with sound effects. This mental imagery, usually involving people, represents either a personal journey or an experience on the part of the dreamer.

There have been many theories about the role and purpose of dreaming. One theory, with the widest following, is based on Freud's original work of sleep and dreaming. Sigmund Freud, the father of psychoanalysis, believed in dreams as mechanisms for reducing our psychic tensions while awake, as well as allowing fulfillment of our unconscious wishes. This popular theory holds that dreams represent *the royal road to the unconscious*, possibly reflecting immediate or past experiences, and helping us resolve some of these conflicts.

A far more pragmatic and certainly less romantic view is that dreams represent a process of *reversed learning* and is therefore simply a method for unloading stored memories and purging unneeded information.

These movies of the mind can be vivid, sometimes with associated sounds and tactile feelings. Tastes and smells while dreaming are rare. Dreams range from being well organized, rational reproductions of life experiences to bizarre, disconnected, irrational images.

Nightmares, representing bad dreams with a powerful emotional content producing anxiety or terror, are unpleasant experiences, affecting sleepers of all ages. These seemingly long and frightening dreams often awaken the sleeper and may be related to some traumatic event or unpleasant incident.

One theory holds that these bad dreams are the result of oxygen deprivation to the brain during sleep, based on recollections of many dreamers being crushed, suffocated or unable to breathe during these nightmares.

Dreaming occurs almost exclusively during periods of

REM sleep. For this reason, REM sleep is also called *D-sleep*. You will see therefore, in subsequent chapters, how snoring relates to REM sleep and why a change in either the pattern or frequency of dreams can be of immense diagnostic value in treating a severe snorer.

We now know that the sleep cycle is directly related to snoring. For evidence of this, we need to correlate sleep and the anatomical structures that actually produce the unwanted sounds of snoring.

## The Source of the Noise

Earlier, we defined snoring as a "repetitive, resonant noise produced by vibrations of the uvula and soft palate during sleep." Other structures, including the tonsillar pillars (strips of tissue around the tonsils), the tongue base, uvula and throat walls all contribute to this sound.

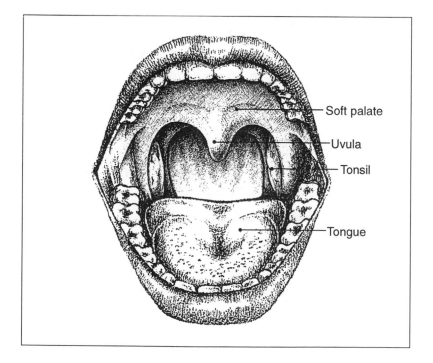

The thin edges of the soft palate, however, sometimes called the *velum*, are the predominant source of the noise. According to Professor Ian Robin, who did extensive research by filming the movements of these structures during sleep, the velum produces a flutter-valve effect, much like a saxophone reed set in motion.

This mechanical sequence of events was eloquently described by Professor Robin in a presidential address to the Royal College of Surgeons in England, as long ago as 1967. The professor remarked that despite an enormous body of literature on dreams, sleepwalking and bed-wetting, only a few articles had appeared in the medical and lay press on snoring. In an effort to correct these omissions, Professor Robin wrote several scientific papers on this subject. Although demonstrating a very thorough understanding of the underlying mechanisms and causes, he had, at that time, very little to offer the snorer. In fact, he remarked that, "treatment to obtain a cure for snoring may not be possible. I hope that further research will enable more of the afflicted to be helped."

As we breathe in during sleep (we call this *inspiration*), air flows through our nose and mouth on its way to our lungs. Without realizing it, every time we inhale, we actually produce a negative pressure in our chest cavity, sucking air into our lungs.

This low pressure change has a suction effect on the soft tissue structures of the upper air-passages. In fact, each time we breathe, the throat walls are pulled inward, much like a drinking straw collapsing when we suck forcibly on it.

The soft tissues of the upper airway are sometimes referred to as the *collapsible airway*. By collapsible, we mean that these structures have no rigid framework or support.

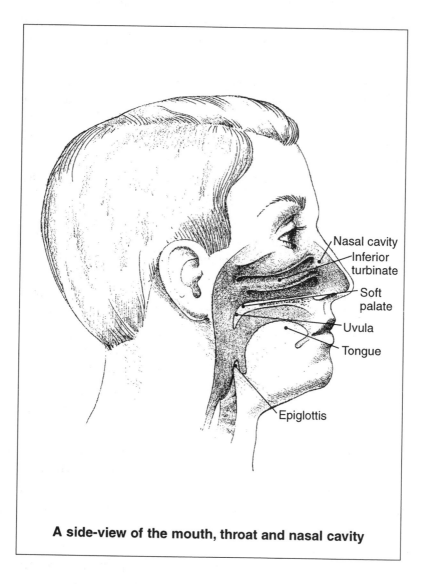

**A side-view of the mouth, throat and nasal cavity**

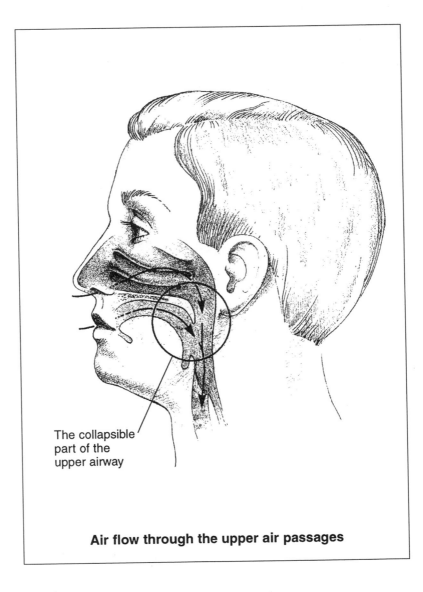

The collapsible
part of the
upper airway

**Air flow through the upper air passages**

However, we would not be able to breathe quietly and efficiently if our throat passages closed up with every breath. We believe, therefore, that certain muscles counteract this collapsing quality of the throat, actually holding these air-passages open. Under normal healthy circumstances of quiet breathing during sleep, this phenomenon is called the *balance of forces*.

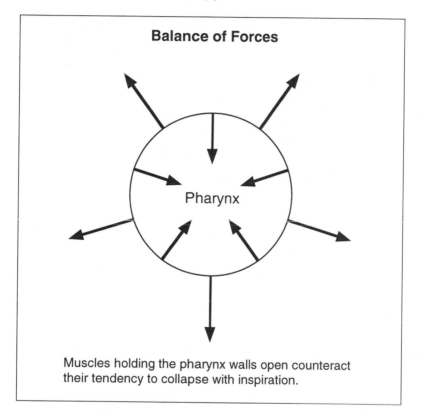

**Balance of Forces**

Pharynx

Muscles holding the pharynx walls open counteract their tendency to collapse with inspiration.

Any narrowing of these air-passages makes us work harder at breathing while we sleep, pulling air in with greater velocity. According to a physical law called Bernoulli's Principle, increased air flow through a hollow tube (in this case, the nose and throat) produces a corresponding drop in pressure, pulling the throat walls inward. Being pliable tissues, they rebound and vibrate, giving rise to the familiar sounds of snoring every time we breathe.

The flutter-valve effect we have described can be likened to a flag snapping back and forth in a stiff breeze, or the loose edge of a sail on a sailboat, luffing in the wind. Any turbulence in the airflow increases this effect.

We can now understand how *any* factor producing even slight narrowing of the upper air passages can cause snoring. Similarly, any condition adding to the slackness of the throat tissues and muscles may have a similar effect.

Ironically, sleep, especially those deep levels of sleep—that state of supposed quiet and relaxation—actually sets the stage for snoring when the conditions are right.

## Why Do We Snore?

With our understanding of the underlying mechanisms, the various causes of snoring and their association with sleeping now become clear.

**Narrowing of the upper air-passages.** Any increased bulk in the soft tissues of the throat effectively narrows the airway by taking up space. This, as we have learned, encourages snoring. Large tonsils or adenoids for example, occupy space in the air passages; bulky neck tissues in some heavyset individuals have a similar effect.

Much of our understanding of these anatomic factors is attributed to the diligent work of a Japanese physician, who rightfully deserves the title, "Father of Snoring". Dr. Takenosuke Ikematsu dedicated his practice in Noda City, Japan, to snoring patients. Between 1952 and 1991, more than 25,000 snorers from all over that country sought evaluation and treatment. Keeping meticulous records, Dr. Ikematsu developed a system he called *mesopharyngometry*. By measuring various internal dimensions of the throat, he could correlate these measurements with degrees of snoring. This system of observed pharyngeal changes in habitual snorers includes one or several of the following:

- An elongated uvula.
- Lowering or drooping of the soft palate.
- Prominent tonsillar pillars.
- Enlargement and thickening of the uvula.
- Large tonsils
- Narrowing or *funnelling* of the back of the throat.
- An enlarged tongue.

Dr. Ikematsu discovered that more than 90 percent of perpetual snorers demonstrated one or more of these anatomic changes. The wide variety of sizes and shapes seen within the mouths of habitual snorers allow us to now understand that *any* obstructing tissue or loose vibrating structure can be associated with snoring. (See diagram on following page.)

Many adult snorers have enlarged, fleshy tonsils, often associated with a long or swollen uvula and a prominent

# The Ikematsu System for the Diagnosis of Snoring

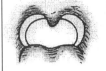

Natural Type

Elongated uvula

Enlarged uvula

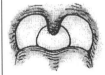

Parallel type

Webbed type

Large tongue dorsum

Tonsillar hypertrophy

Shallow oropharynx

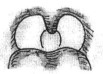

Posterior arch narrowing

Bifid uvula

Imbedded type

Emerging type

Anterior arch narrowing

Wide soft palate

Hypertrophy of the lateral pharyngeal folds

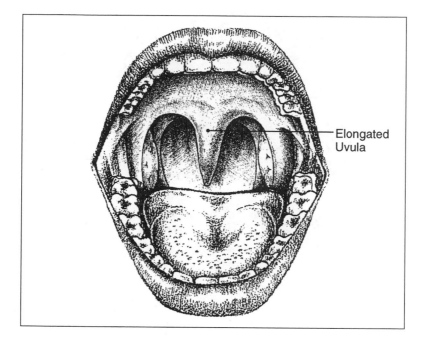

Elongated
Uvula

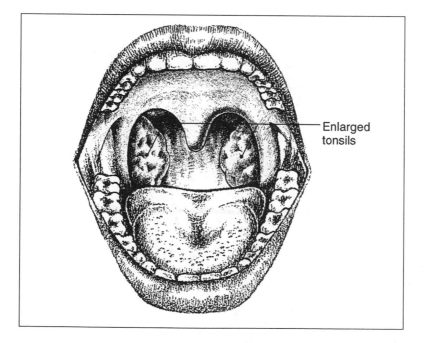

Enlarged
tonsils

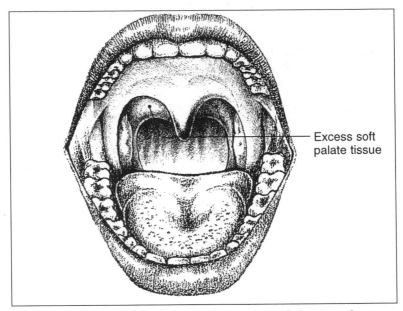

Excess soft palate tissue

tongue. We refer to this combination of throat obstructions from above, below, and the sides as *crowding of the pharynx*. In addition, a receding chin causes the tongue to protrude into the back of the throat, partially blocking the airway.

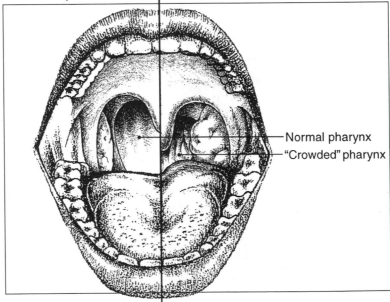

Normal pharynx
"Crowded" pharynx

However, some habitual snorers, in good general health, may have perfectly normal throat anatomy without displaying any of these described obstructive changes, making the riddle of snoring ever more complex.

**Reduced muscle tone in the tissues of the throat.** Muscle relaxation increases with the depth of sleep. The more relaxed the tissues, the greater the likelihood of vibration—and the sounds of snoring. As we have seen, maximum muscle relaxation occurs during REM sleep—especially in the neck muscles. Most snoring occurs, therefore, during this period of deep sleep. Lying on your back aggravates the situation because your tongue customarily falls backwards into the upper airway due to relaxation of muscles in this area, augmented by the pull of gravity. This further narrows the airway, forcing greater air-flow over the already relaxed throat tissues.

Muscle tone in these tissues decreases with age as the elastic content of these structures diminishes. This process, which eventually affects all of us, makes the tissues of our upper airway more floppy and less resilient, even in our waking state. It isn't surprising then that snoring increases significantly as people get older. Similarly, a number of medical conditions associated with decreased muscle tone, including an underactive thyroid or Down's syndrome, are often accompanied by snoring.

**Snoring and Weight Gain.** Many snorers are somewhat overweight. Although the exact mechanisms by which obesity causes or aggravates snoring are unclear, we do have several ideas. Collections of fat may compress and narrow the throat. A thick neck and double chin frequently seen in an obese person has a similar effect. In addition, overweight individuals are invariably flabby and out of condition. Finally, increased collections of fat in the abdominal cavity can push up the diaphragm and compress the wind-pipe.

Some valuable research on the close association between weight gain, snoring and sleep-related breathing disorders is currently being conducted by Paul Suratt, M.D., Director of the Sleep Disorders Clinic at the University of Virginia Medical Center.

He has clearly shown the benefit of supervised weight loss for these conditions. He has demonstrated, however, that loud snoring, developed before weight gain, will usually not be cured by weight loss alone.

**Drugs, Fatigue and Smoking.** Tranquilizers, sleeping pills, antihistamines or alcohol, taken in excess and prior to sleep, can aggravate snoring by deepening a person's sleep and causing greater than normal relaxation of upper airway tissues. Fatigue, overeating or overwork can also exaggerate the conditions leading to snoring, by resulting in over-relaxation of airway muscles and tissues.

Smoking, though not a direct cause of snoring, contributes to it by producing excess mucus and causing the membranes in the throat to swell and restrict the air-passages.

**Can snoring be inherited?** Snorers frequently ask whether their habit is hereditary. Although no "snoring gene" has ever been identified, snoring can certainly run in families because we inevitably inherit specific physical characteristics from our parents. These could include anatomic variations in the size or shape of your neck, throat or nose—factors commonly associated with snoring.

Aside from all these factors, any obstruction in your nasal passages can contribute to snoring when that obstruction is coupled with the changes your body undergoes as you switch over to automatic pilot during sleep.

So why don't we simply work around this nasal obstruction by breathing through our mouth?

## Why We Persist in Nasal Breathing

First, even though you breathe through your mouth as well as your nose, there seems to be some instinctive desire to breathe through the nose anyway—even when the nostrils are severely obstructed. For example, think of the discomfort you go through with acute nasal congestion from the 'flu or a cold. You can breathe perfectly well through your mouth during these times, yet you frantically seek out an effective nasal decongestant. One reason for this curious phenomenon is that you actually increase the work of breathing when you breathe through your mouth, bringing on physical fatigue as well as psychological anxiety.

Second, studies show that resistance in the oral airway is actually greater than resistance in the nasal airway when we are lying down, asleep. During sleep, the nasal airway seems to be the body's preferred route for breathing, compared with the path of higher resistance when breathing through our mouth. To understand this, we have to return to our discussion of the anatomical changes occurring during the stages of sleep.

During normal sleep, the firmness of your throat muscles slackens, the airway narrows and increased resistance to inspiration follows—because the passageway through which your breath must pass is reduced. This normal collapse of your throat tissues as the muscles relax, restricts the space in your upper airway, bringing the soft tissues more directly into the path of your breath.

Breathing-in power (we call this *inspiratory pressure*) must increase in order to counteract this natural narrowing of the upper airway during sleep. As the sleeper's effort to breathe increases, greater pressure is exerted on the soft tissues of the pharynx, pulling them inward. As a result, these tissues start vibrating forcibly with each breath.

With a congested nose, the sleeper is required to breathe entirely through his mouth. This narrows the air passage even more, as air passing into the throat directly from the mouth produces a negative pressure in the back of the throat, exerting suction on the soft tissues of the collapsible airway.

You can re-create this effect while awake by lying down, and, with your mouth closed, breathe slowly and deeply through your nose. If there's no obstruction, the air should pass through effortlessly. Now, hold your nose closed and breathe slowly and deeply through your mouth. You should be more aware of air passing over your collapsible tissues; you should also feel these tissues being pulled in slightly as the air creates a vacuum. Current research suggests that the firm bone and cartilage structures supporting the nasal airway prevent this vacuum effect when you breathe through your nose.

## Common Nasal Causes of Snoring

If nasal obstruction causes disturbances in normal, wakeful breathing, then it's not surprising that such obstruction complicates nighttime breathing and contributes to snoring. Just knowing the possible causes of nasal obstruction is of great value in determining whether or not you snore and where you might begin to look for factors that bring it on. For example, hay fever might cause snoring without ever being identified as the culprit. If the sufferer is lean and fit, is a nondrinker and a nonsmoker, he might futilely resign himself to his snoring as some quirk of nature, never realizing that it's due to his seasonal allergies.

Similarly, a pregnant woman might become confused and embarrassed when she suddenly begins to snore. If she realizes that nasal congestion is a common occurrence

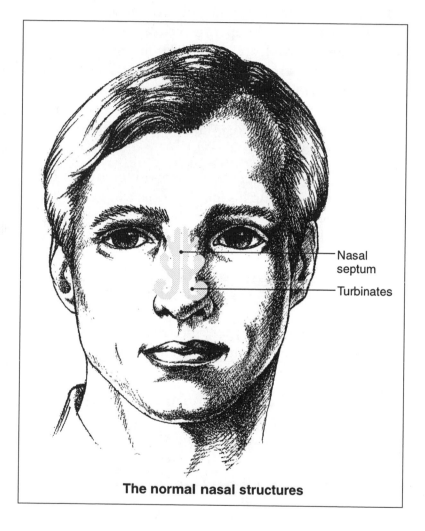

Nasal septum

Turbinates

**The normal nasal structures**

in the early stages of pregnancy, and may be the reason she breathes through her mouth, she will be more at ease.

Here are some of the many nasal causes of snoring commonly encountered in an ear, nose and throat practice:

**Infection:** Acute or chronic infections frequently cause nasal obstruction. Viral upper respiratory tract infections, like the common cold, are usually self-limiting, ending in a couple of days, so that snoring may be temporary. Bacterial infections of the nose and sinuses, however, may cause persistent congestion and pressure in the head and face, usually accompanied by increased nasal secretions with postnasal drip.

**Allergy:** Approximately one person in ten suffers from allergic reactions during his life. Seasonal allergies, such as hay fever, are caused by sensitivity to grass, tree, flower and weed pollens drifting through the air at certain times of the year. Perennial allergies (to house dust or cat hair and the like) usually produce persistent nasal congestion, accompanied by copious watery secretions and bouts of sneezing.

Most upper respiratory allergies result in swollen mucous membranes inside the nose and consequently, obstructed nasal breathing; hence snoring.

**Drugs and medicines:** Aspirin, oral contraceptives and estrogens—to name but a few medications—can bring about endocrine changes affecting the nasal air passages. Tobacco, as we now know, irritates the mucous membranes, impairing the protective action of the nasal hairs, called *cilia*. Decongestants (drops and sprays) can clear up the nasal airway, but relief is usually temporary. Repeated use actually irritates the membranes, creating further nasal obstruction. With each application the user benefits less from the decongestant, leading to increased dosage or frequency of use, or both. As a result, the user can become a "nose-spray addict."

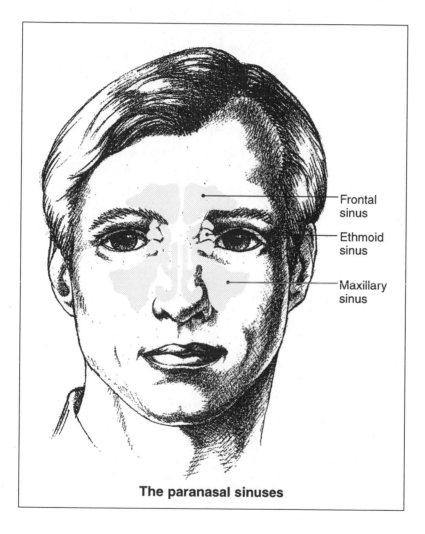

Frontal
sinus

Ethmoid
sinus

Maxillary
sinus

**The paranasal sinuses**

A number of drugs used to treat high blood pressure can also lead to chronic nasal congestion and obstruction.

**Irritants:** Continuous exposure to such occupational irritants as dust, fumes or to environmental pollution can create inflammation of the mucous membranes in the nasal airway and thus, nasal obstruction. We call this *occupational rhinitis*. While we are beginning to realize the severity of the irritants around us, correcting the damage we've done to our air is an issue that will always demand monitoring and control.

**Vasomotor rhinitis:** This condition, which frequently brings patients into my office, is blamed on an imbalance in the *autonomic* (automatic) nervous system controlling blood flow through the mucous membranes of the nose. In other words, fine balance in the neural control of the mucous membrane somehow becomes disturbed through such factors as position, humidity, temperature, exercise or emotion. The result is swelling of structures inside the nose, called *turbinates*. Symptoms of *vasomotor rhinitis* are similar to those of allergies, with persistent congestion and excessive drainage. The exact cause of vasomotor rhinitis is unclear, though the condition is often seen in people suffering from depression, chronic emotional stress or anxiety.

**Growths and swellings:** Obviously, tumors in the nose or sinuses, or enlarged adenoids can contribute to nasal congestion and obstruction; one of the early symptoms may be increased snoring.

**Anatomic deformities:** Among the most common conditions seen in this category include a deviated nasal septum (often attributed to previous injury) and nasal polyps, both of which can produce significant nasal obstruction.

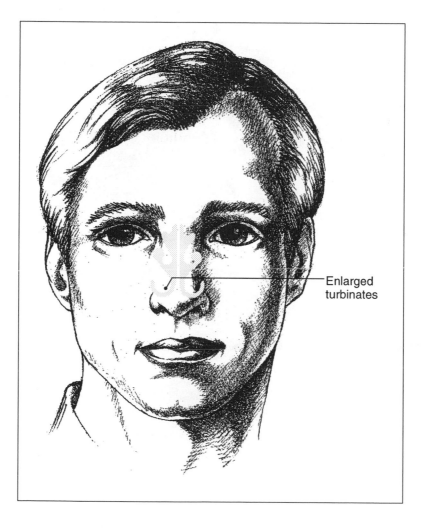

Enlarged
turbinates

The nasal septum is a bony and cartilaginous partition separating the two sides of the nasal cavity. Injury to the septum or asymmetrical growth during childhood can cause buckling of these structures, resulting in nasal obstruction.

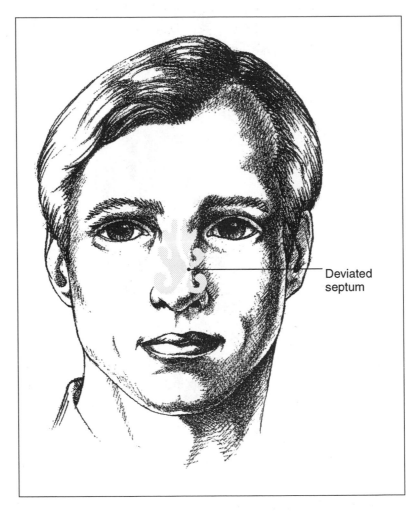

Deviated septum

Nasal polyps are swellings arising from the mucous membranes of the nose and sinuses. These pale, grape-like masses tend to produce progressive nasal obstruction as they continue to grow inside the nose. Obstruction can range from partial to complete; frequently there is secondary infection in the sinuses, resulting in symptoms of chronic headache and postnasal drainage. We suspect that most polyps have an allergic basis.

**Nasopharyngeal lesions:** A variety of obstructive tumors can arise from the area behind the nose called the *nasopharynx*. These lesions usually cause progressive nasal obstruction. Other symptoms may include bleeding, pain, postnasal drainage and, of course, snoring.

## Why Do Men Snore More?

Throughout this investigation into the causes of snoring, one constant is that snoring occurs far more commonly in men than in women. Although these numbers vary according to the research, snoring is approximately ten times more common among men. But why?

We suspect that men have a greater tendency to build up bulky throat tissues which then become filled with fat, getting softer and more relaxed as they age, and therefore, set the stage for snoring. As males gain weight, they do so by depositing fat around their abdomens, necks and shoulders. These male characteristics are largely due to the action of a male hormone (androgen) which stimulates appetite, weight gain and salt retention—all of which can aggravate snoring.

Physicians recognize the profile of a typical snorer as a large, heavily-built man in his forties or fifties who has gained weight and neglected regular exercise. There are, of course, many exceptions to this stereotypical portrait. In medical practice, for example, we frequently see fit and trim young patients whose habitual honking has caused them to be thrown out of campgrounds!

Female patterns of fat distribution, sad but true, inevitably produce weight gain around the hips and thighs, thus avoiding fat-loading of the neck and protecting the integrity of the upper airway. In addition, a female hormone (estrogen), is thought to protect against the development of severe snoring in women by stimulating respiration. This is born out by the fact that the incidence of women snorers definitely increases after menopause.

Despite the gender characteristics that obviously produce more male than female snorers, women are certainly not immune. In the past, women may have appeared somewhat reluctant to acknowledge a snoring habit because it's regarded as an unfeminine trait. Now, however, they readily seek advice and treatment when their snoring appears to threaten a relationship.

In summary, any factor constricting your upper respiratory airway, bringing the collapsible tissues into greater contact with the air flow or adding to the slack of these tissues can cause snoring—because snoring is the sound produced when these tissues vibrate uncontrollably and rapidly as we breathe.

## Summer Snoring is the Loudest

Each year, the coming of summer transforms many bedrooms into noisy torture chambers, according to modern snore-lore. The reason: Scientists have shown that men snore louder and longer during the shorter nights of summer than they do in winter, and the fault lies with the sun. Longer days mean more chance to absorb ultraviolet rays from the sun, which produces more relaxation at bedtime. The more relaxed, the more vigorous the snoring.

Recognizing the causes of snoring represents not only a breakthrough in the field of sleep medicine, but a valuable contribution to the well-being of snorers everywhere. When we understand causes, we can start to identify cures. And in that critical transition from causes to cures, snorers can be released from the frustrating world of gadgetry and bromides, bringing them into the scientific world of sound medical diagnosis and treatment.

Before we come to a discussion of that world, however, we must first understand the numerous side-effects of snoring in order to decide *when* medical attention is required for the snorer, and what sort it should be. Medical science has now come to realize that understanding and treating snoring can sometimes be much more than merely treating a social annoyance—it can be saving a life!

# Chapter 3

# Sleep Apnea:
# The Darker Side of
# Snoring

For some people, snoring can be much more than mere bedroom sound-effects; it can be the signal of real trouble! It is sometimes the most obvious sign of an un-detected, yet potentially serious medical condition.

Admittedly, not *all* the effects of snoring are serious. This amusing but pointed snore story appeared in the *New England Journal of Medicine:*

A 66-year-old man came to visit Neil Shear, M.D., of Toronto, complaining of pain and tenderness in his right calf. Finding no obvious cause for these symptoms, the doctor prescribed painkillers to help his patient through the next few days, telling him to come back if the pain became worse. "Several nights later," as Dr. Shear reported in his letter to the *Journal,* "the patient had just fallen asleep when he was awakened by a sharp pain in the right calf, caused by a kick from his wife."

"Don't kick me there," he said. "That's just where my leg hurts."

"You were snoring again," she answered, "and that is where I always kick you to stop it."

The wide variety of symptoms associated with snoring are often just as mysterious as this patient's calf pain. In fact, sleep disorders specialists throughout the world demonstrate every day that snoring is not simply an isolated, irksome quirk, but may, in many cases, be connected in some way to an underlying medical problem.

## Tired from Snoring

In 1984, physicians in a medical clinic in Washington, D.C., studied the experiences of severe adult snorers and their partners. As expected, these accounts included such complaints of, "drives my wife from the bedroom" and "my girlfriend won't marry me." Similar colorful anecdotes included, "Grandpa's snoring is a big joke to our grandchildren;" "he shakes the entire house;" and "he's no longer invited along on hunting or fishing trips."

But such comments as, "falls asleep on the job;" "naps while watching TV;" "is drowsy all day;" and "falls asleep while eating dinner," were more intriguing from a medical viewpoint. These symptoms suggest that snoring is more than merely a bothersome sound, but is somehow related to excessive tiredness.

It was hardly the first time that sleepiness had been associated with some other medical condition. In 1837, in *The Posthumous Papers of the Pickwick Club*, Charles Dickens told of the very fat boy Joe, who fell asleep and was "snoring feebly," while standing perfectly upright and knocking on a door. This character portrayal ultimately found its way into the medical literature. Nearly a century later, Sir William Osler, a renowned physician and professor of medicine at Johns Hopkins Medical School, coined the term *Pickwickian* for those obese patients exhibiting excessive sleepiness.

According to Dr. Osler's astute clinical observations, "an extraordinary phenomenon in excessively fat young persons is an uncontrollable tendency to sleep, like the fat boy in Pickwick".

But the correlation between sleepiness, obesity *and* snoring had yet to be made.

## When Snoring Takes Your Breath Away

In 1965, the first report to make this connection appeared in the medical literature. This paper told of an obese patient who complained of constant tiredness and sleepiness during the day—and was a heavy snorer. His snoring was associated with periods when he would stop breathing. This led to the realization that some patients previously diagnosed with *narcolepsy* (a sudden, irresistible need to sleep) suffered instead from episodes of obstructed breathing while sleeping, followed by excessive daytime sleepiness.

Based on these observations, Dr. Elio Lugaresi, a respected sleep researcher, in 1972 proposed the term *hypersomnia with periodic apnea* (*apnea* meaning a cessation of breathing) for this condition. As an alternative description, he offered the more colorful *la maladie du gros ronfleur* (the illness of the heavy snorer).

Then, in 1975, at an international conference on sleep disorders, *sleep apnea* was finally chosen as the universal term for this condition. Tribute for clarification of this complex disorder of the upper airway must be paid to Dr. Christian Guilleminault, a pioneer sleep researcher and currently director of the internationally renowned Sleep Disorders Center at Stanford University School of Medicine. Dr. Guilleminault and his research team studied breathing patterns in several hundred habitual snorers with daytime tiredness, comparing them with normal subjects. They concluded that although occasional breath-holding during sleep was seen in many healthy people, those fatigued snorers all held their breath for periods upwards of 10 seconds, recurring many times during sleep.

These observations led the Stanford group to derive the term *apnea index*, referring to the number of apneas recorded during each hour of sleep.

During these early days of sleep research, some snorers were found to take very shallow breaths during sleep, rather than have complete cessation of respiration. Researchers referred to this partial breathing obstruction as *hypopnea*. *Apnea*, however, is not a new word. It is derived from the Greek, meaning literally "for want of breath".

Snorers aren't the only people who experience periods of sleep apnea. Brief apneas of up to 10 seconds also occur during the sleep of healthy nonsnorers, from infancy through adulthood. Occurring fewer than twenty to thirty times during the night, these apneas are usually considered normal, being more likely to increase with age, or when alcohol or sedatives are consumed before going to bed.

## Wake Up, Dear—You're Choking!

Snoring and sleep apnea do not necessarily develop hand in hand. Severe habitual snoring is usually considered a step in the evolution of sleep apnea. However, once the constant snoring pattern is established, there is usually a progression in the severity of snoring as well as an increase in the number of times the snorer stops breathing during the night. With each of these repeated apneas, the sleeper becomes increasingly short of oxygen. These are the moments which send the snorer's companion into a panic— the snorer appears to have stopped breathing! In fact, that's exactly what happens.

When normal breathing resumes, the snorer overcomes the choking consequences of sleep apnea and goes back to sleep, only to have the entire sequence repeat itself. In severe cases, these episodes can occur hundreds of times throughout the night.

In virtually all cases of obstructive sleep apnea, the back of the throat is the primary site of this obstruction. At some point, while sleeping, inhalation causes the soft tissues of the throat to collapse sufficiently to create airway obstruction. This area is normally narrowed during sleep by the combined effects of muscle relaxation, mucous membrane congestion, and the tongue falling backwards, from gravity.

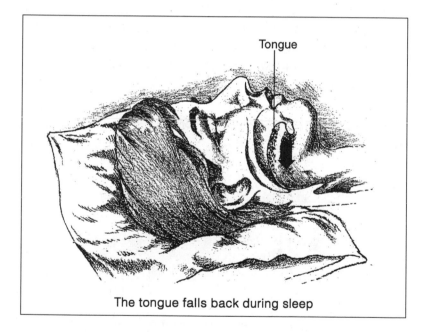

Tongue

The tongue falls back during sleep

Anatomic changes in the upper airway, such as enlarged tonsils or a bulky tongue can further the development of sleep apnea, although many patients with this problem *do not* necessarily have obvious obstructions in their throats. However, several of the described factors contributing to snoring are usually present in sleep apnea patients. In addition, many of these patients are overweight.

We don't know exactly how obesity affects the upper airway, but we do know that there is strong external pressure on the walls of the throat in those who have very thick necks. The floppy, easily collapsible pharynx in heavyset and heavy-snoring patients shows their snoring to be an intermediate stage between normal breathing during sleep and the early stages of sleep apnea.

Aging also produces flabbiness in the soft tissues of the upper airway, and combined with stretching from years of habitual snoring, these tissues eventually collapse sufficiently to obstruct your airway.

Finally, as described earlier, any nasal obstruction can cause an additional vacuum-effect in the back of your throat when you inhale. It's as if you were sucking the air out of a paper bag.

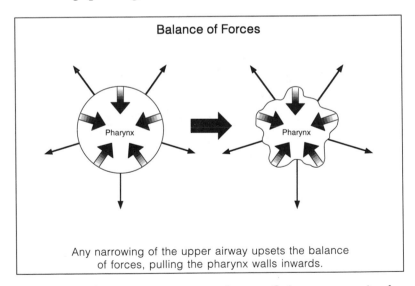

Balance of Forces

Any narrowing of the upper airway upsets the balance of forces, pulling the pharynx walls inwards.

By far, the most common form of sleep apnea is the result of blockage or obstruction in our upper air passages; we therefore refer to this as *obstructive sleep apnea*, abbreviated as *OSA*.

A far less frequent variation of sleep apnea known as *central apnea*, is the result of the breathing center in our brain temporarily "shutting down". Simply put, we forget to breathe! These events rarely occur spontaneously; central sleep apnea occurs in association with severe obesity or with diseases of the central nervous system such as polio or multiple sclerosis, causing extreme muscle weakness.

Occasionally, both obstructive sleep apnea and central sleep apnea may coexist. Under these circumstances, we apply the term *mixed apnea*.

As you will learn, *obstructive sleep apnea* produces many symptoms. This medical condition, therefore, is referred to as the *obstructive sleep apnea syndrome* (OSAS). A *syndrome* is an associated group of symptoms and clinical signs characterizing a disease or disorder. For reasons of clarity, the term *sleep apnea* and its abbreviation *OSA* will be used throughout this book, rather than the more unwieldy *obstructive sleep apnea syndrome*.

## How Your Body Handles Sleep Apnea

When a snorer stops breathing during an episode of apnea, a number of chemical changes take place in his body. The oxygen level in his blood starts to drop (this is known as *hypoxia*), and the carbon dioxide level rises (*hypercapnia*), along with the degree of acidity in his blood (*acidosis*). The effect on breathing is the same as if his head were being held under water.

The level of oxygen in the blood of a snorer experiencing sleep apnea decreases as the duration of obstruction in his upper airway increases. Of course, any chronic disease or thickening of the membranes in the snorer's lungs—such as seen in heavy smokers or asthmatics—compounds the oxygen shortage which occurs during each apneic event.

A rising level of carbon dioxide in the snorer's body during apneic episodes triggers that part of the brain controlling respiration, briefly awakening the snorer in order to overcome the breathing obstruction. This arousal period lasts a matter of seconds and is reflected in brainwave changes, hence the term *micro-arousal.* And the sleeper usually doesn't know that he has momentarily awakened. And even if he does know he is awake, he doesn't realize that it was due to a biological, lifesaving action. His anxious partner if often wide awake by now, nervously following the changing patterns—severe snoring . . . silence . . . breath holding . . . a deep gasp (called the *resuscitative snort*) . . . restless body movements . . . falling back into a deep sleep—snoring resumes. And this cycle repeats itself many times throughout the night.

A snorer's sleep becomes fragmented by these recurring micro-arousals, which may occur hundreds of times during the night. Ironically, although these awakenings help get the snorer breathing again—and thus save his life—they seriously interfere with the quality of his sleep. Imagine how you would feel in the morning if your telephone rang throughout the night, waking you every 10 or 15 minutes. Researchers believe that this *sleep fragmentation/sleep deprivation* and interruption of the rapid eye movement (REM) phase of sleep, accounts for many of the physical problems which characterize the obstructive sleep apnea syndrome.

Someone with a history of heart disease, for example, can further aggravate that problem if he develops sleep apnea. The reduced oxygen and increased carbon dioxide levels which inevitably follow, affect the sleeper's heart and blood vessels.

Slowed heart rates and abnormal heart rhythms, as related to low oxygen levels as well as to acid-base changes in the blood, can sometimes lead to heart attacks and even cardiac arrest during sleep. If the snorer also suffers from narrowing of blood vessels to the heart (*ischemic heart disease*), then sleep apnea puts him at severe risk during the night. Long-standing sleep apnea, for the same reasons, may impair function of the heart muscles, ultimately causing cardiac failure.

When a large number of patients with established sleep apnea were studied, more than half were found to have high blood pressure. This elevated pressure (*hypertension*) initially appears to correspond with decreased blood-oxygen levels during the obstructive breathing events.

Essentially, your heart has to work harder while breathing stops. In many cases, however, this raised blood pressure continues into waking hours. As a result, a sleep apnea sufferer is now faced with the additional risks of possible stroke or heart disease, associated with prolonged hypertension.

## Diagnosis: Insomnia—Wrong!

The wake-response following periods of apnea is often associated with restless arm and leg movements. These fitful sleep interruptions resulting from reduced levels of oxygen and REM sleep contribute to many of the symptoms of sleep apnea, including daytime sleepiness, mood changes, memory loss, and depression. Unfortunately, for the already suffering snorer, the symptoms resulting from sleep apnea are sometimes misdiagnosed as insomnia.

However, sleep apnea frequently develops so insidiously that the associated fatigue may be attributed to merely getting older. Apnea sufferers, when prompted, seem to have little difficulty describing their symptoms. Some of the most vivid comments include, "Doc, I wake up every morning with a hangover even though I haven't been drinking," or "after a full night's sleep, I wake up feeling more tired than I did before I went to bed".

Morning headache is another common complaint among sleep apnea sufferers. Physicians attribute this to

The chain of medical events in established sleep apnea.

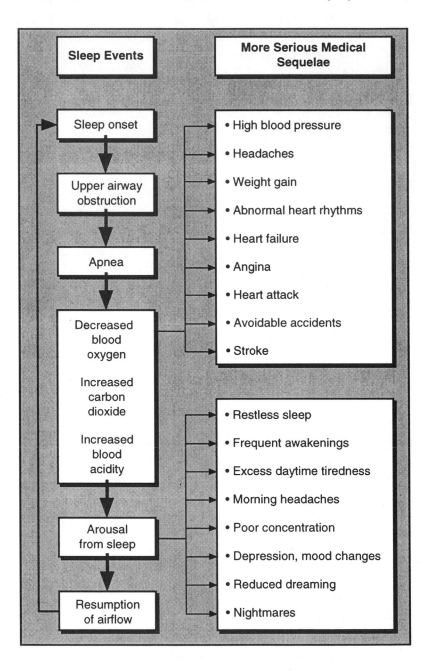

sustained high blood pressure or the dilating effects on the blood vessels around the brain, resulting from abnormally high levels of carbon dioxide in the blood during recurring apneas.

Approximately 80 percent of those with obstructive sleep apnea admit to becoming very sleepy during the day. We believe this is due to the reduced oxygen levels (*hypoxia*) and sleep deprivation/ fragmentation escalating with the obstructed breathing at night, and producing symptoms such as mood swings, decreased intellectual function and depression.

Together with these mental and emotional changes, the physical incapacity produced by excessive daytime sleepiness (*hypersomnolence*) often causes the snorer problems at work, invites automobile and occupational accidents and can lead to difficulties in marriage and other relationships.

One of my patients admitted driving 20 miles past his freeway exit because he had somehow put himself on automatic pilot behind the wheel. But perhaps the most remarkable example of hypersomnolence is the Las Vegas dealer who fell asleep, snoring uncontrollably between poker hands, oblivious to the noise and excitement of the casino. Regrettably, these symptoms are frequently misdiagnosed as psychological rather than physiological in origin.

---

### Business Billed for Sleep Disorders

Sleeping problems in the workplace—whether the result of irregular shifts or medical disorders—are costing companies an estimated $70 billion annually in lost productivity, huge medical bills and avoidable industrial accidents. Sleep disorders, of course, are particularly frightening in areas affecting public safety. Researchers say that as more is learned about the economic toll of sleep disorders, companies will find they cannot afford to continue ignoring the problem. Megabucks are involved, and sometimes, lives.

*The Wall Street Journal (July 7, 1988)*

---

## Two Sleepy People

It was business as usual on a Saturday night at Clancy's, a popular restaurant in New York's Greenwich Village—until a middle-aged couple fell asleep at the table between their entree and dessert, snoring loudly, to the obvious discomfort of surrounding diners.

"Excuse me," said the waiter quietly, bending over to wipe crumbs from their table. The woman awoke briefly; her husband napped on.

Another waiter appeared, bearing samples of dessert. The couple finally awoke, ate their chocolate mousse and nodded off again, oblivious to the laughter around them. Onlookers began to whisper. Were they narcoleptics? Were

# Tips for Drowsy Drivers

More than 30 percent of highway accidents are related to driver fatigue. Here are some tips to avoid these pitfalls:

♦ Have the courage to pull over as soon as you feel drowsy behind the wheel.

♦ Avoid driving soon after lunch or dinner; there is a natural tendency to sleepiness after a meal.

♦ Be sure to get plenty of rest before long driving trips.

♦ Avoid any alcohol while driving. Even one or two drinks can make you sleepy, especially when you have been sleep-deprived before a driving trip.

♦ Many medications, including decongestants, tranquilizers, muscle relaxants, some pain pills and even blood pressure medication can increase your level of sleepiness. Read the labels very carefully; avoid driving if your medication seems to make you even slightly drowsy.

♦ Seek medical help immediately if you suspect any type of sleep disorder associated with excess daytime tiredness.

Remember, most driving accidents related to driver fatigue can be avoided. You can help make the road a safer place for all!

they simply bored with each other? How could anyone nod out in the middle of an expensive dinner?

With just enough time to say, "My check, please," the man was snoozing again, this time over his credit card.

The owner strolled over, tactfully placed a gentle hand

on the sleeper's shoulder, and asked, "Did you enjoy your meal, sir?"

The man's eyes fluttered open. "Yes, very much," he said. The tired couple made it to their feet, retrieved their coats, and left the restaurant as if nothing out of the ordinary had happened.

## Your Problems Are Not Yet Over

Sleep apnea sufferers frequently report that they rarely dream any more. This paucity of dreaming stems from repeated interruptions of REM sleep. As we have learned, our dreams occur during REM, the deepest levels of sleep, previously referred to in the medical literature as *D-sleep*.

This alteration in the pattern and frequency of dreaming is of diagnostic value in evaluating sleep apnea. When their apnea is treated and REM sleep restored, patients often describe the return of long, vivid dreams. It's as if they are now making up for lost time, restoring the richness of a dream-laden sleep.

Many male snorers with sleep apnea may experience impotence. This personal and delicate subject is a complex one, with numerous contributory causes, both psychological and physical. Sleep researchers, studying impotence in sleep apnea patients, ascribe this to the cumulative effects of chronic fatigue, depression, weight gain, high blood pressure and the aging process. Additionally, the loud snoring which invariably accompanies sleep apnea frequently forces the snorer or snoree to seek separate bedrooms. Finally, new research has discovered lowered male hormone levels in both obesity and sleep apnea.

As you can now understand, this package doesn't exactly make for romance! The good news is that with successful treatment, many snorers with sleep apnea can return to the bedroom, enjoying the warmth and intimacy of a renewed sexual relationship.

## Sleep Apnea Results in Fuzzy Thinking

Problems in performing intellectual skills also plague long-time sleep apneics. For example, *The Wall Street Journal* reported the experience of Robert Legan, an industrial physicist who slept poorly over several years and, in the interim, lost the ability to solve abstract problems as well as he once could. "I'd be trying to construct an equation, and I'd have to go look in books," he said. "And even then, I'd have a hard time figuring out these things that I'd known two years before." Subsequent examination at a sleep disorders center revealed that Legan suffered from severe sleep apnea.

Unfortunately, we still don't know how often snoring leads to sleep apnea. "We know that in this country," says David Fairbanks, M.D., of George Washington University School of Medicine, "about one person in eight snores.

We don't know what percentage of snorers will eventually develop sleep apnea. We believe that apnea affects between two and three million people across the country, and that

## Does Snoring Cut into Intelligence?

According to the results of an experiment conducted by A. Jay Block M.D., snoring can interfere with your intelligence and your ability to think and act when awake.

Dr. Block's findings, presented at a meeting of the American Society of Chest Physicians in Anaheim, California, in 1985, centered on heavy snorers, recruited in an effort to determine the effect of oxygen deprivation on the brain. Each subject was hooked up to appropriate instruments during the night. The following morning these subjects were divided into three categories: Those who never stopped breathing and never dropped their oxygen level; those who did so occasionally; and those who did so excessively.

Intelligence quotient, memory and verbal fluency all dropped in direct proportion to their oxygen deprivation. In other words, those who stopped breathing most frequently during the night scored the lowest on tests given the following day for intelligence, reaction times and visual coordination.

"I don't want to say that snoring makes you stupid," Dr. Block concluded, "but you may not be able to accomplish your whole potential. It may make you a little less smart."

It is significant that the majority of subjects tested were students or professors—people ordinarily required to function at a high intellectual level.

every year two or three thousand people die in their sleep because of it."

During episodes of sleep apnea, the complete absence of airflow through the nose and mouth lasts for at least 10 or 15 seconds, and periods of 30 to 40 seconds are not unusual. In severe cases, they may last as long as 60 seconds, or even longer. Apnea sufferers are alarmed, even horrified, to see these recordings on their sleep tests, frequently remarking that they cannot hold their breath for anywhere as long while awake.

The explanation is that the body's oxygen needs during sleep are lower than in the awake, active state. It's analogous to the low gasoline consumption of an idling automobile compared with the increased gas usage of a car speeding down the freeway.

But many snorers don't experience apnea, and some *nonsnorers* may have sleep apnea. A large group of patients diagnosed with sleep apnea at Stanford University Sleep Disorders Clinic showed the following distribution of symptoms: 96 percent snored very loudly; 44 percent experienced excessive daytime sleepiness; 24 percent were depressed; 36 percent demonstrated reduced intellectual function; 56 percent were hypertensive; 23 percent admitted to impotence; and 8 percent suffered from *enuresis* (bed-wetting).

Unfortunately, records show that apnea during sleep is far more common among the general population than experts once thought. In 1988, researchers at Uppsala University in Sweden mailed 4,064 questionnaires concerning sleep habits, snoring and hypersomnolence to a random sampling of men aged 30 to 69 in one municipality. Of the 3,201 who responded, 690 admitted to habitual snoring; 236 experienced significant daytime sleepiness.

In the second phase of this study, 156 of these men

were invited for overnight sleep testing, based on the severity of their symptoms. Sleep studies were eventually done in 61 respondents, confirming sleep apnea in 15. Applying these statistics to the general population, these researchers concluded that at the lower limits, sleep apnea affects 1.3 percent of men in Sweden between the ages of 30 and 69—representing more than 25,000 people in that country.

Another two-phase investigation into the prevalence of sleep apnea associated with hypersomnolence among industrial workers in Israel produced similar results. Although questionnaires were sent to workers of both sexes, all the positive respondents were male. This study concluded that more than 3 percent of the country's male industrial workers were afflicted with sleep apnea.

## When Lifestyle Leads to Snoring... and Apnea

Misdiagnosis of sleep apnea in adults can have an equally profound effect on the health and psyche of the sufferer. Consider the case of Peter Jones, a 57-year-old executive, who lived his life in the fast lane. His days were filled with corporate meetings and long-distance phone calls. Lunches were often three-martini, high-pressure affairs with corporate directors and executives of other companies.

Peter awoke with a dull headache every morning, but had learned to live with it. Afternoons, however, were difficult for him. Returning to the office after lunch, he would nod off and have difficulty concentrating. Evenings were even worse. Peter had numerous social commitments—charity events, dinner parties and activities at his country club—where alcohol flowed freely. He often caught himself drifting off to sleep during the after-dinner speeches.

Peter's hectic pace left him little time for exercise, other

# Some Startling Statistics on Obstructive Sleep Apnea

♦ Approximately 3,000 people die in their sleep every year from causes directly related to obstructive sleep apnea (OSA).

♦ Two-thirds of people with sleep apnea have high blood pressure; one-third of people with high blood pressure have OSA.

♦ A tip for drowsy drivers: The second most common cause of driving fatalities, after alcohol, is excessive sleepiness. The risk is especially high for those with sleep apnea; this risk is heightened by the fact that this condition often goes undiscovered only until after it causes a serious accident.

♦ Sleep-related disorders produce an estimated $70 billion loss to businesses every year from accidents, medical bills and lost productivity.

♦ People with untreated sleep apnea have a seven times greater incidence of automobile accidents than members of the general population.

than an occasional Sunday golf game. And this was usually followed by drinks and dinner at the club.

When Peter returned home at night, he invariably fell into a deep sleep accompanied by severe snoring, an added source of marital stress in a relationship already strained by his frequent absences. Peter's wife had taken to sleeping in a spare room so she could get a good night's rest.

Peter's sedentary life began to show in weight-gain. This produced even more snoring, worse morning headaches and more daytime sleepiness.

Finally, realizing that both his health and his marriage were failing, Peter consulted an internist who diagnosed "overwork", encouraging him to eat and drink more sensibly, started him on an exercise program and prescribed a mild tranquilizer.

Although his weight dropped, Peter's symptoms worsened. His search for a diagnosis eventually brought him to a lung specialist with a special interest in sleep medicine. He recognized the symptoms of a sleep-related disorder in Peter, realizing that the tranquilizers were aggravating his condition.

With successful treatment, Peter's suffering and accompanying despair were happily resolved.

## On the Brink of Sleep Apnea

As sleep research progresses, some important new information has emerged concerning the association between snoring and tiredness.

We can now identify an interesting group of patients who seemingly have sleep apnea—loud snoring at night associated with extreme daytime sleepiness. However, testing these patients for sleep apnea has proven negative. Forty-eight patients fitting into this category were studied at the Stanford University Sleep Disorders Clinic. Surprisingly, their overnight breathing tests were completely normal. In other words, each patient had a normal *respiratory disturbance index* (RDI). (This test will be discussed in detail in a later chapter.)

These patients proved to be something of a diagnostic puzzle. Looking more closely at their brain-wave patterns, however, the researchers noticed that instead of smooth, deep sleep, they observed short bursts of arousal waves, occurring in relationship to alterations in their breathing. Rather than holding their breath for long periods, as we see in sleep apnea, these patients experienced very brief periods of breath-holding and shallow breathing.

Introducing a special breathing machine called *continuous positive airway pressure* (much more about this later), brain-waves were restored to normal. More important, their daytime sleepiness resolved completely.

This valuable research has led us to now understand that some patients who, in the past, had been diagnosed with a type of narcolepsy called *spontaneous hypersomno-*

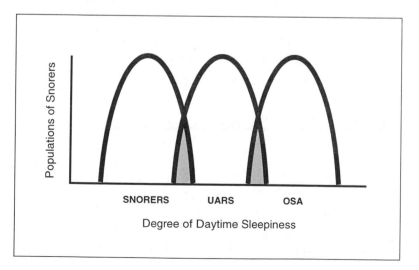

*lence*, in fact, have a breathing problem at night. We now refer to this incipient or threshold version of obstructive sleep apnea as the ***upper airway resistance syndrome***.

This partial closure of the upper airway at night, which typically precedes complete obstruction, seen in OSA, is now referred to in the medical literature as *inspiratory flow limitation*.

Thanks to some innovative thinking by the Stanford University sleep researchers, we can now identify an ever-expanding number of snorers with daytime sleepiness, who qualify for treatment. Physicians now regard the *upper airway resistance syndrome* (UARS) as a transitional stage between heavy, habitual snoring and established sleep apnea, with identical attendant symptoms and potential complications.

## Snoring and Sleep Apnea in Children

A snoring child is frequently a source of alarm to parents—and an annoyance to a brother or sister sharing the bedroom. As in adults, snoring in childhood signals an obstruction in the breathing passages of the nose or throat. And, as we have seen in adults, loud habitual snoring in children may progress to frank obstructive sleep apnea.

Anatomical obstruction in the upper airway from enlarged tonsils and adenoids is among the most common causes of snoring and apnea in children. Abnormalities in a child's facial skeleton, especially a small or recessed jaw, reduced muscle tone (as with Down's syndrome) and chronic nasal obstruction (from allergy or infection) can all contribute to their obstructed breathing.

Sleep apnea frequently has a profound effect on the quality of a child's life, influencing personality, behavior, mood, learning ability and general physical development. Parents often describe these children as restless sleepers who are difficult to arouse, being disoriented and con-

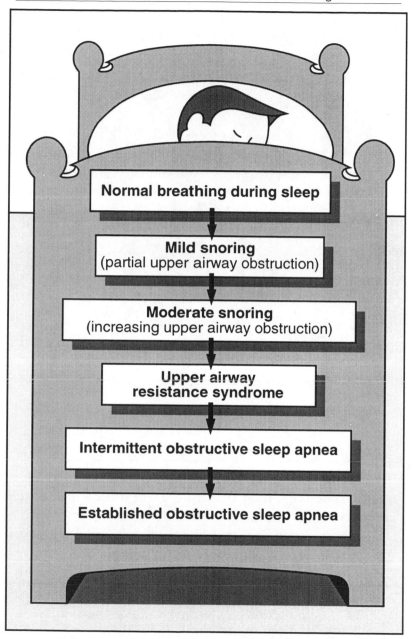

**Normal breathing during sleep**

**Mild snoring**
(partial upper airway obstruction)

**Moderate snoring**
(increasing upper airway obstruction)

**Upper airway
resistance syndrome**

**Intermittent obstructive sleep apnea**

**Established obstructive sleep apnea**

fused when awakened. Changes in the intellectual ability of these children are common—attention lapses and inability to concentrate—for which they might be punished because of their behavior, is mistakenly regarded as day-

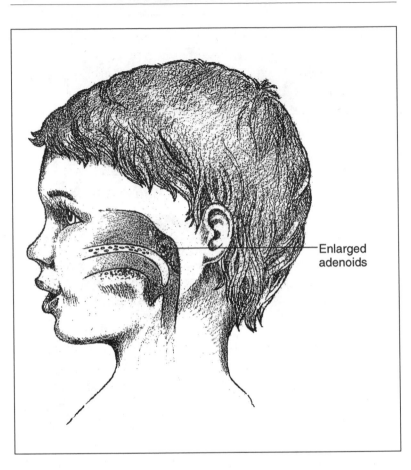

Enlarged
adenoids

dreaming or indifference. Older children, who have the ability to describe their symptoms, will sometimes voluntarily complain of morning headaches.

Unlike their adult counterparts, snoring children with disturbed sleep are usually not overweight. On the contrary, they tend to be thin and below their expected height and weight. These children may also be bed-wetters—usually due to a reduction in muscle tone as a child drifts into deep levels of sleep after numerous awakenings.

As with adults, children with sleep apnea may have many associated symptoms which are either missed or misinterpreted by their pediatrician or family doctor. For example, poor weight gain and low energy levels are not unusual in some children; and learning difficulties accompanied by a drop in school performance have myriad causes.

Interestingly, this problem was highlighted in a recent article in *The Washington Post*, discussing a survey of pediatricians' training in childhood sleep disorders. A team of researchers from the Medical College of Pennsylvania and New York Hospital-Cornell Medical Center, conducted a three-part assessment. First, they surveyed 158 of the nation's 215 pediatric residency programs to determine whether they offered elective or required courses in sleep disorders. They then sent a true/false quiz on sleep to Philadelphia pediatricians; 88 doctors responded. Finally, they conducted a survey of 183 pediatricians in Rhode Island and Pennsylvania, questioning their knowledge about sleep problems among children and adolescents.

These researchers' findings reinforced the conclusions drawn by the National Commission on Sleep Disorders Research in 1990, reporting that physicians are taught too little about sleep problems. The research team found that pediatric residency programs offer an average of less than five hours of instruction on sleep disorders, problems which are believed to affect at least one in every four children. They found that many pediatricians continue to prescribe ineffective and potentially dangerous treatments such as sedatives and tranquilizers to promote sleep, rather than investigating the underlying problem. Nearly half the pediatricians surveyed told concerned parents that children "always outgrow their sleep problems".

A review at Stanford University Medical School of 100 children with confirmed sleep apnea sheds light on the wide variety of problems this condition introduces into a child's life. Seventy-three of these children had excessive daytime sleepiness noted by parents and teachers; more than half of this group had nightmares or night terrors. Seventeen described morning headaches; 58 showed failure to thrive, being markedly underweight for their age. In the older children studied, sleepiness, fatigue and tiredness were apparent.

Special testing identified many with delayed language acquisition and decreased school performance. At least half of this group had frequent coughs and colds; *all* demonstrated heavy habitual snoring—the hallmark of obstructive sleep apnea. Other noted features of their behavior at night included bed-wetting, sleep-walking, profuse sweating and restless sleep, with frequent awakenings.

A closer examination of their personalities revealed some asocial behavior, such as fighting with peers and parents, crying easily, aggressiveness and inappropriate behavior. Most of the children in this Stanford group had a shortened attention span, often with quick shifts from hyperactivity to excess tiredness. Simply put, most of these kids ran out of gas as the day wore on.

By rattling the rafters, junior may be providing parents and pediatricians with valuable clues to the underlying causes of assorted childhood problems such as bad breath, poor appetite, dental caries, open bite and inability to smell.

## Johnny, the Snoring 5-Year-Old

Johnny was a 5-year-old boy whose constant snoring had become the joke of the household—except to his older brother, who had to sleep in the same room.

Johnny looked like a child half his age. He was thin and spindly with dark circles around his eyes. He always seemed tired and without energy, especially in the afternoons and evenings. During dinner, Johnny became irritable and poked along at the table, pushing aside chunks of meat in favor of soft foods and liquids.

His parents had tried a number of remedies, including vitamin tonics and protein supplements, but to no avail. His pediatrician observed enlarged tonsils and adenoids,

PEANUTS reprinted by permission of United Feature Syndicate, Inc.

and referred the young patient to me. Johnny underwent surgery; on his first night home from the hospital he slept quietly for about 12 hours. Within a few months, he gained weight, had much more energy during the day, no longer had dark circles around his eyes and regained his former pleasant disposition.

## Does Mary Really Have Attention Deficit Disorder?

Without question, Mary was one unhappy camper! This six-year-old girl was a burden to her parents as well as her teachers. She arrived at school each day looking tired and unhappy. Her irregular behavior had become disruptive to the rest of the class; to her teachers, she appeared sullen and uncooperative.

Mary was barely able to focus her attention on any project such as drawing or coloring before giving up, displaying temper tantrums or teary outbursts. She would constantly fidget and squirm in class. Her apparent mood swings and lack of energy did not encourage friendships with her classmates, leading to more sulking and withdrawal.

According to her parents, Mary would readily fall asleep in the car on the way home from school; on weekends she would nap at odd hours during the day. Her constant snoring and restless sleeping habits had long been of concern to her parents.

Consulting a school psychologist, Mary's behavior was interpreted as attention deficit/hyperactivity disorder (**ADHD**); she was placed on Ritalin, with the consent of her pediatrician. Although her attention span seemed to improve along with her general school performance, her moodiness and antisocial behaviors did not change to any great extent.

# When to Suspect Sleep Apnea in Childhood

## WHILE ASLEEP

♦ Loud snoring, punctuated with recurring periods of silence.

♦ Constant mouth-breathing with restless sleeping.

♦ Disturbed sleep—restless movements, unusual body positions, frequent awakenings.

♦ Extreme thirst during the night.

♦ Bad dreams and nightmares.

♦ Difficult to arouse.

♦ Bed-wetting (enuresis).

## WHILE AWAKE

♦ Lethargic and slow to get going on awakening.

♦ Developmental delay, poor concentration, inattention and moodiness.

♦ Excess daytime sleepiness.

♦ Morning headaches.

♦ Constant mouth breathing.

♦ Slow eating with poor appetite.

♦ Thin and underweight for age.

♦ Dry mouth and bad breath on awakening.

Seeking another opinion, Mary's parents consulted a children's lung specialist who diagnosed a sleep-related breathing disorder. Once this was corrected, Mary's mood improved, her attention and hyperactivity problems resolved, allowing her to participate in all the normal social activities that she had previously shunned.

**The ADHD Epidemic:** We have seen a dramatic increase in the incidence of attention deficit disorders during the past decade. Since 1990, the number of children diagnosed with ADHD has risen disturbingly from approximately 800,000 to almost 4 million. This suggests a problem of almost epidemic proportions. ADHD appears to be more common in boys; 1994 data estimates that 5 percent of boys and 1.5 percent of girls had been labeled as having attention deficit by their physicians.

The most widely prescribed treatment for ADHD is Ritalin, an amphetamine derivative, hence a stimulant. The rapidly increasing frequency with which the diagnosis of ADHD is made has produced a concomitant increase in Ritalin prescription and usage. In fact, since 1991, there has been a 700 percent increase in Ritalin prescriptions for children of school-going age.

This explosion in amphetamine prescribing seems to be unique to North America. Statistics from other countries including Canada, Australia and Great Britain show that the rate of Ritalin usage remains approximately one-tenth that of the USA. Attention deficit/ hyperactivity disorder has become something of a boutique diagnosis in the United States. By this, we mean that it is apparently fashionable to readily stigmatize with this condition *any* child who displays shortcomings in academic performance or exhibits unruly behavior at home or school.

True attention deficit/hyperactivity disorder *must* be distinguished from other transient behavioral problems of childhood. In other words, the diagnosis of ADHD should be made by a qualified professional, following accepted medical guidelines. Many of the symptoms of attention deficit/hyperactivity are described in a publication of the American Psychiatric Association, *A Diagnostic and Statistical Manual of Mental Disorders:*

### Inattention
- Often fails to give close attention to details or makes careless mistakes.
- Often has difficulty sustaining attention in tasks or play activities.
- Often does not seem to listen when spoken to directly.
- Often fails to complete school work, duties, chores.
- Often has difficulty organizing tasks and activities.
- Often reluctant to engage in tasks requiring sustained mental effort.
- Often loses things needed for tasks (pencils, books, tools).
- Often easily distracted by extraneous stimuli.
- Often forgetful in daily activities.

### Hyperactivity
- Often fidgets and squirms.
- Often leaves seat when remaining seated is expected.
- Often runs, climbs, moves excessively when inappropriate.
- Often has difficulty in playing quietly.
- Often "on the go", constantly moving.
- Often talks excessively.

To meet the accepted criteria for ADHD, any child must show at least six out of nine symptoms of inattention or at least six of nine behaviors indicating hyperactivity. Other criteria should include:

- Symptoms begin before age 7.
- Child must demonstrate problem behaviors in several situations (home and school).
- Behaviors must cause impairment in functioning.
- Behaviors cannot be better explained by other conditions.

Concerned parents need to understand that there is no single reliable test for ADHD. Rather, children who are suspected of having this condition must fulfill these diagnostic features.

A closer look at many comparable aspects of ADHD and sleep-disordered breathing in childhood (obstructive sleep apnea and the upper airway resistance syndrome) reveals a disturbingly high number of shared symptoms. Parents frequently voice concern about their hyperactive child's insomnia and restless sleep; researchers studying ADHD have often considered these features to be results of the underlying behavior disorder (or its treatment) rather than a contributory cause.

Recent studies by Ronald Chervin, M.D. at the University of Michigan show a link between inattention, hyperactivity and sleep-disordered breathing. Habitual snoring was found in 33 percent of children diagnosed with ADHD, but only in 10 percent of children in comparative groups. Similarly, snoring and excess daytime sleepiness were associated with higher levels of inattention and hyperactivity.

Data from this research suggests that by control of sleep-related breathing disturbance, establishing normal sleep patterns, ADHD could be eliminated in a large percentage of those children with attention deficit *and* habitual snoring.

Research by David Gozal, M.D. at Tulane University School of Medicines goes one step further by examining the association between sleep-disordered breathing and school academic performance in first and second graders. This recently published study clearly demonstrates a correlation between sleep-breathing problems and learning ability. Furthermore, treatment (in most cases, removal of tonsils and adenoids) resulted in significant improvement in school performance. On the basis of these findings, this researcher recommends that sleep-related symptoms should be actively sought in all children with learning difficulties or developmental problems, ensuring timely evaluation and appropriate treatment.

These clinical studies raise a number of thought-provoking issues:

♦ Can sleep-breathing disorders in childhood masquerade as ADHD?

♦ How often does ADHD and obstructive sleep apnea (or its variants) coexist in young children?

♦ When these conditions do coexist, how will the correction of one component influence future behavior and performance?

♦ How many children have been incorrectly or prematurely diagnosed with ADHD when their essential underlying problem is sleep-related?

♦ Can numerous children (to say nothing of parents and teachers) be liberated from their daily ration of Ritalin?

♦ What are the long-term sequelae (side-effects, drug habituation) of regular amphetamine usage?

Clearly, further research is needed to shed light on this ubiquitous childhood medical problem, having such a serious social and economic impact on millions of families nationwide. And pediatric residency training programs across the United States are now emphasizing the possible existence of a sleep disorder as the underlying cause of any child's deficiencies in general health, development or performance.

## The Serious Side of Snoring

Because snoring continues to be thought of as a nuisance rather than a medical problem, getting to the appropriate medical specialist is not always easy. The associated high blood pressure, impotence, depression, mood swings and other described symptoms are all too often misunderstood by the snorer or misdiagnosed by the physician. Years may be spent in futile attempts to fit square pegs into round holes. It is now patently clear why sleep apnea is called "the darker side of snoring".

Understanding that snoring is now regarded as a legitimate medical symptom is the first step out of that cycle. The next step is to obtain the needed medical help, when appropriate. To do this effectively, every snorer needs a clear idea of how bad their snoring really is. You need a quick, reliable test, to be taken on your own, to determine your snoring level and whether or not there are any associated features of sleep apnea. In other words, you need to know your Snore Score . . .

# Chapter 4

# What's Your Snore Score?

Physicians who once dismissed snoring as little more than a hopeless nuisance now know better. Thanks to recent evidence provided by sleep researchers throughout the world, they are now convinced that severe snoring is more than simply a social handicap, but rather, a legitimate medical problem which can be treated. With this new attitude toward an old condition, we can begin providing answers to questions that once were unanswerable:

- How severe is my snoring?
- How loud does it actually get during the night?
- What does it mean if: I choke and gasp between snores? My snores are punctuated by long periods of silence? I sleep fitfully, kicking out my arms and legs? I wake up feeling exhausted?
- When should I seek medical advice?
- When should I start to worry that my snoring might

be associated with sleep apnea? Or that the sleep apnea might be a real health hazard?

I developed the following questionnaire to help you and your partner resolve these and some other concerns you may have. I realize that it may be embarrassing to admit to loud snoring and even more difficult to admit to constant tiredness or depression. For most men, it may be downright humiliating to discuss their own impotence. And many women are reluctant to come right out and say that they snore outrageously. Such subjects do, after all, intrude into a most intimate and private area—the bedroom. But it is important that you be completely frank in giving your answers.

I encourage you to think of the time you spend on this questionnaire as an opportunity to discuss a shared health concern with your partner. The purpose, after all, is to examine a personal medical condition with a view to obtaining help.

## The Snore Score Questionnaire

Using the following scale, answer the questions by circling a number that most appropriately describes your situation: 1 . . . never; 2 . . . very infrequently; 3 . . . occasionally; 4 . . . often; 5 . . . always or almost always.

---

## Snoring

1.  How often have you been told that you snore?                      1 2 3 4 5

2.  Does your snoring disturb your bedroom partner?                 1 2 3 4 5

3.  Does your snoring disturb others in the next room?             1 2 3 4 5

4. Do you snore constantly through-
   out the night?                        **1 2 3 4 5**

5. Do you snore only when you sleep
   on your back?                         **1 2 3 4 5**

6. Do you snore when you sleep in
   all positions?                        **1 2 3 4 5**

7. Have you been told that you stop
   breathing for long periods
   between snores?                       **1 2 3 4 5**

8. Has your snoring ever caused you
   to wake up suddenly?                  **1 2 3 4 5**

9. Does your bedroom partner leave
   the room to sleep elsewhere
   because of your snoring?              **1 2 3 4 5**

10. Has your snoring caused you so-
    cial embarrassment on vacations?
    At conferences? In motels?          **1 2 3 4 5**

---

**Comments:** If you scored 3 or more on questions 1 through 4, your snoring almost certainly interferes with your personal life. With a score of 4 or more on questions 6, 7 and 8, there's a likelihood that you experience periods of apnea during your sleep. You should therefore consult a physician.

If your answer to question 5 indicates that you snore *only* when sleeping on your back, your snoring is probably due to the effect of gravity on the tissues of your upper airway rather than to any anatomical obstruction. You are what we call a *positional snorer*. Remedies that encourage you to sleep on your side or stomach may be sufficient.

If you scored 4 or more on question 6, your snoring is more than likely a result of some physical obstruction. You should see a physician for an examination of your upper airway.

A score of 4 or more on *all* questions in this section also indicates that sleep apnea is very likely. You should consult a physician with a view to an overnight sleep study so that your snoring and sleep behavior can be observed and evaluated.

## Sleep Habits

1. Does it take you a long time to fall asleep at night?      1 2 3 4 5

2. Do you wake up during the night?      1 2 3 4 5

3. Do you wake up before you've had a full night's sleep, unable to return to sleep?      1 2 3 4 5

4. Have you ever awakened choking or gasping for breath?      1 2 3 4 5

5. On awakening, do you still feel tired?      1 2 3 4 5

6. Is it difficult for you to awaken and get out of bed after sleeping?      1 2 3 4 5

7. Do you make frequent arm or leg movements during sleep?      1 2 3 4 5

8. Do you have bad dreams or nightmares?      1 2 3 4 5

**Comments:** Questions 4 through 7 deal with symptoms frequently associated with obstructive sleep apnea. If you score highly on these questions *and* are a heavy snorer, I suggest you seek medical advice, and, if deemed appropriate, undergo an overnight sleep test. The remaining questions in this section are inconclusive for sleep apnea specifically, dealing instead with sleep habits in general. However, if your answers are positive to most or all of the questions, you probably have an underlying medical condition adversely affecting the quality of your sleep. If this is the case, I suggest you seek appropriate medical attention.

# Excessive Daytime Sleepiness

1. Do you feel tired during the day? 1 2 3 4 5

2. Do you need to nap during the day? 1 2 3 4 5

3. Do you fall asleep watching television, in church or at the movies? 1 2 3 4 5

4. Have you ever fallen asleep while working (during a meeting or while operating machinery, for example)? 1 2 3 4 5

5. Do you experience drowsiness while driving? 1 2 3 4 5

6. Have you ever been in a motor vehicle accident because of drowsiness while at the wheel? 1 2 3 4 5

7. Have you noticed any recent unexpected moodiness or increased irritability? 1 2 3 4 5

8. Are you aware of difficulty in concentrating or keeping your thoughts on track? 1 2 3 4 5

**Comments:** As with the preceding section, *excessive daytime sleepiness* (EDS) is not, in and of itself, an absolute indicator of sleep apnea. Any cause of reduced oxygen levels in the blood—such as fever and pain, heart failure or emphysema, for example—can bring about daily fatigue.

One prominent cause of daytime sleepiness is *narcolepsy*. Those who suffer from this central nervous system disorder have a higher incidence of sleep apnea than occurs in the general population. Alcohol and other drugs (stimulants or depressants) can interfere with every level of sleep, resulting in sleep deprivation/ fragmentation and increased daytime sleepiness. Of course, psychological conditions, such as anxiety and depression, can also result in sleep loss, leading to daytime fatigue. The disorders of excessive sleepiness are numerous and therefore require accurate medical diagnosis.

If your scores in the previous two sections indicate a strong likelihood of sleep apnea, then high scores in this section should further support your suspicion of this condition. You should therefore seek medical attention, since your sleep habits may be harmful to your health.

---

## Lifestyle

1. Are you a moderate to heavy smoker?                    1 2 3 4 5

2. Do you eat large meals shortly before going to bed?          1 2 3 4 5

3. Do you have a nightcap (alcohol) before going to bed?        1 2 3 4 5

4. Is your snoring worse after those occasions when you've had several drinks?          1 2 3 4 5

5. Do you exercise regularly?          1 2 3 4 5

6. Do you take tranquilizers, sedatives, decongestants or stimulants?          1 2 3 4 5

7. Do you drink large amounts of caffeinated beverages (coffee, tea, cola)?          1 2 3 4 5

8. Are you within your recommended body weight?          1 2 3 4 5

9. Has your snoring increased as a result of weight gain?          1 2 3 4 5

10. Does impotence disrupt your sex life?          1 2 3 4 5

---

**Comments:**

**Question 1:** Smoking is known to irritate the mucous membranes of your airway. This causes swelling and increased mucus production—both of which add to obstruction of the upper airway, causing snoring or making it worse.

**Question 2:** A lot of energy is required to digest large meals, especially food rich in protein. Blood is diverted from your intestines to aid in digestion. This brings on a heavier sleep, resulting in increased muscle relaxation, which aggravates snoring. A distended stomach from overeating can interfere with movement of the diaphragm, reducing respiratory movement, and contributing to sleep apnea.

**Questions 3 and 4:** Alcohol is a potent central nervous system depressant, promoting muscle relaxation and upper airway collapse. It also depresses your arousal response to reduced oxygen levels. This can precipitate a severe snorer into obstructive sleep apnea or aggravate the condition in one who already has it.

**Question 5:** Through exercise you increase and maintain muscle tone; this can overcome the tendency of the upper airway tissues to collapse.

**Questions 6 and 7:** Tranquilizers, sedatives and decongestants are all central nervous system depressants, having the same effect on snoring and apnea as alcohol does. Stimulants (such as caffeine) can interfere with your normal sleep cycle, often causing insomnia. When restful sleep finally comes, it tends to be deeper, accompanied by greater muscle relaxation, which encourages snoring.

**Questions 8 and 9:** There is a very strong correlation between snoring and weight gain. Furthermore, many sleep apnea sufferers are overweight. The mechanisms by which excess weight affects snoring and apnea are discussed in earlier chapters.

**Question 10:** Research shows that a substantial number of patients with sleep apnea suffer from a reduced sex drive and impotence. Scientists think it's due to the combined effects of repetitive oxygen reduction, fatigue and depression associated with sleep apnea.

If you score 3 or more points on most questions in this section, *and* you are a loud habitual snorer, there is every likelihood that your lifestyle is standing in the way of your snoring . . . and your health.

## Snorer, Be True to Yourself!

By now, you and your partner should have a better understanding of the snoring that disturbs your nights. In previous chapters we examined the anatomic, physiologic and behavioral factors which contribute to snoring. We have also acknowledged that loud constant snoring is, in many cases, not simply a social nuisance, but, in fact, one symptom of a medical condition posing a real threat to your health.

Admittedly, your snore score questionnaire responses cannot provide a *complete* answer to all your concerns. But these quiz results should make you more familiar with your sleep habits and their possible medical implications. This should help prepare you to consult with a physician when appropriate, and to understand what issues he or she will examine, as well as how they will be considered.

Your next step is to obtain medical advice. This can often be a daunting task, so let's discuss how to enter the medical system in search of answers . . . and where to begin.

# Chapter 5

# Selecting a Physician:

## Finding Dr. Snore-No-More

If you snore severely or are the partner of someone who does, and you feel that some kind of help is needed to curb the constant noise, you can now choose from a number of medical specialists trained for the job.

During the past decade, a new specialty called *sleep disorders medicine*, has arisen. It is practiced by physicians interested in the medical problems affecting our bodies when we switch over to automatic pilot during sleep. These physicians are usually drawn from the fields of pulmonology, neurology, otolaryngology and sometimes psychiatry. They frequently work together as a team for the benefit of patients with sleep-related breathing disorders.

Generally, patients consult first with their family physician or internist when they have a medical problem. Too often, unfortunately, these doctors are unaware of the latest developments in treating sleep disorders. Until recently, medical schools rarely dealt with this subject in any depth.

A 1978 study showed that fewer than 10 percent of United States medical schools provided *any* education in the area of sleep medicine. A mere decade later, a national survey among 126 medical schools showed only a modest increase in teaching hours allocated to this subject. Thirty-seven institutions reported one or fewer hours of classroom education about sleep and its disorders during the first two years of medical school.

As I look back over my own medical education, I cannot remember the word "snoring" ever being mentioned at medical school, during internship or throughout my five years of residency training to become an ear, nose and throat specialist.

Once in practice, it was no wonder I was so insensitive to the anguish of wives complaining bitterly about their husband's snoring. Like so many of my colleagues, I blithely passed the matter off by telling these women that if they really loved their mates, they would have to live with their problem. We've all come a long way since then!

## The Winds of Change

Changes have occurred to some extent in our nation's medical school courses, with lectures and discussions on sleep apnea and other sleep-related problems now being included in classes on pulmonary medicine or as part of a neurology rotation.

The American Thoracic Society recently conducted a survey about sleep disorders training in pulmonary medicine (lung diseases) fellowship programs. Nearly 70 percent of programs surveyed maintained an active sleep laboratory. Of those programs without a sleep lab, the majority had alternative arrangements to teach fellows in training about sleep disorders.

Articles on sleep medicine now appear with increasing regularity in medical journals and publications, informing primary care physicians about advances in this field. Popular magazines and newspapers such as *Reader's Digest, Time, People* and *The Wall Street Journal* have all recently published articles on this topic.

One logical place to begin solving any serious snoring problem is with a physician having a special interest in sleep-related breathing disorders. This may be a medical subspecialist in the field of pulmonary or neurological medicine, or an ear, nose and throat surgeon. Today, however, in the climate of managed health care, your primary care physician should be the point of entry into this medical system. Ask your family physician or internist for the names of appropriate physicians who can treat snoring and sleep apnea. If he or she can't help you, your local medical society or hospitals should have the information you seek.

While all ear, nose and throat physicians are familiar with upper airway problems, not all are familiar with the modern treatments available for snoring and obstructive sleep apnea. Some of these physicians, for example, specialize in children's ear disorders, while others restrict their practices to cosmetic facial surgery. You need to find out whether the physician to whom you are referred is prepared to treat snoring and related problems.

## That First Phone Call

Once you've located the appropriate physician, don't attempt to conduct an extensive interview over the telephone. Here is why doctors don't welcome such a discussion during your initial call:

**Medical reasons:** To give any medical advice, a physician must have a firm grasp of the patient's individual health history and specific clinical findings. This cannot be acquired through one phone call.

**Professional reasons:** Few health questions have quick and easy answers; you will want to speak at some length with the physician about your problem. But the patient who is in the office by appointment may be understandably annoyed if his or her time is interrupted frequently by extended telephone calls.

**Legal reasons:** The current climate of litigation makes physicians wary of providing detailed information over the telephone to people they have never seen. For example, a lawyer might call on behalf of a hostile insurance company, but not identify herself as such. Or a patient may want to gain information that could be used against another physician.

What *can* you do? Call each physician on your resource list and ask the receptionist the following questions:

- Does Dr. _____ evaluate and treat snoring and sleep apnea?

- Does Dr. _____ work in conjunction with a sleep disorders center or offer unattended sleep monitoring?

- Is Dr. _____ familiar with the medical and non-surgical treatments for snoring and sleep apnea?

- Has Dr. _____ performed many surgeries for snoring?

- Does Dr. _____ incorporate a medical laser into his/her practice?

- If Dr. _____ is a medical specialist, does she work in association with a surgeon trained in the modern surgical procedures for treatment of snoring and sleep apnea?

If the answers to these questions indicate that the physician has an interest and involvement with sleep problems, then, using whatever other criteria are relevant for you—location, insurance, availability—make an appointment for a consultation.

## The Previsit Questionnaire

Before your first visit, or while in the physician's office, you will be asked to complete a questionnaire regarding your general health and sleep history. This will usually include the following:

♦ Age, sex, weight, height and recent weight gain.

♦ Past medical and surgical history (previous illnesses, surgeries, hospitalizations and current medications).

♦ Personal history concerning diet, exercise, smoking and alcohol use.

♦ Ear, nose and throat history (nasal problems, allergies, infections and previous surgery on the tonsils, nose or sinuses).

♦ Snoring history (loudness and pattern of snoring, the amount of disturbance it causes other family members; recent changes in intensity and pattern of snoring; body positions in which snoring occurs; do the use of tranquilizers, other medications, or alcohol increase the snoring?)

♦ Sleep habits (estimated number of sleep hours, number of awakenings during the night; episodes of choking or breath-holding; changes in dream patterns; and tiredness upon awakening).

♦ Excessive daytime sleepiness (sleepiness which causes constant fatigue, mood change or depression; memory loss, personality change, accidents or unusual sleep behaviors, such as falling asleep readily in church, the movies or the need to take several daytime naps).

## The Consultation—What to Expect

The initial physician's visit is the appropriate time to ask your in-depth questions and to express your concerns. Now you are paying for a consultation. Consult!

Because the first step towards the diagnosis and treatment of your problem is made during this visit, I advise that the snorer's partner accompany him or her to the physician's office. Your companion can provide invaluable information for the doctor by describing your snoring in colorful terms that may not have been voiced before, for example, "earthquake snoring," "mating sea lion snoring" or "buffalo stampede snoring". At this time, your partner can also confirm abnormal sleep behaviors such as breath-holding or restless sleeping.

Snorers are frequently in strong denial of their habit. On many occasions, at the insistence of their mates, men have reluctantly been brought to my office, protesting vigorously that they do not snore. On questioning, however, many of these snorers will admit to sudden awakenings, hearing the tail-end of their snores.

Following a review of your sleep and medical history, your evaluation should also include a complete physical examination—with special emphasis on your blood pressure, heart and lungs—as well as a detailed examination of your upper respiratory tract. These tests are not always conducted by one physician; you should therefore not be surprised if you are referred to other specialists to complete this evaluation. In addition, blood tests will usually be performed and x-rays taken of your chest.

Of course, the study of your upper airway is an important part of this examination. Special attention will be paid to any abnormality or obstruction in your nasal airway, the area behind the nose (*nasopharynx*), your throat, larynx and the region behind your tongue (*hypopharynx*).

Special instruments are required for this part of your

examination, which is usually done by an ear, nose and throat specialist. Using a headlight or reflecting head-mirror, together with a nasal speculum, the physician examines the inside of your nose for obstructions such as a deviated nasal septum, polyps or enlarged nasal turbinates (the bones on the inside walls of the nose). The doctor will then look in your mouth and oral cavity, taking special note of the size of your tongue, the presence of tonsils (their size and any intrusion they make on the airway), length of the uvula and the position of tissue folds in the soft palate on either side of the uvula.

The nasopharynx is examined with either a reflecting mirror or a *fiberoptic nasopharyngoscope*—a narrow, flexible tube which is inserted into your nose after preparing the mucous membranes with a local anesthetic and decongestant. This allows your physician to examine your nasal airway and recesses in the back of your throat, in order to detect any infection or obstructing lesion.

During this part of the examination, you may be asked to perform a *Mueller's maneuver*, consisting of a forced inspiratory effort with your nose and mouth closed. This allows the physician to pinpoint the area of maximum soft tissue collapse. A useful test, of a similar nature, has been described by Dr. Jeffrey Hausfeld, a Washington, D.C. otolaryngologist. Here, you are asked to voluntarily snore while the soft palate is splinted with a fiberoptic laryngoscope. This allows the examining physician to decide whether the uvula and soft palate are the major source of your snoring.

## Searching the Sinuses

We know that nasal congestion can cause or aggravate snoring, and this may also contribute to the development of sleep apnea. Additionally, chronic infection in the air-

**Examination with a fiberoptic endoscope**

containing cavities in the bones of the face and skull (*paranasal sinuses*) can produce symptoms of congestion, increased nasal drainage, postnasal drip and headache. Chronic sinusitis of this nature is sometimes referred to as "the cold that never goes away." More common in cooler climates, sinus infections can affect people of all ages. Attention to the sinuses, therefore, should be an integral part of your upper respiratory examination.

With a flexible endoscope, your physician looks for any nasal obstruction, such as a deviated septum or nasal polyps, which may contribute to sinus disease. He or she also looks for increased secretions in the nose or nasopharynx, as this may be one sign of chronic infection.

In addition, a similar examination of the sinuses may be done in your physician's office by spraying the nose with a decongestant/topical anesthetic solution, using a *rigid* endoscope to visualize areas from which the sinuses drain into the nasal cavities. The optical clarity of this instrument allows your doctor to detect even relatively minor changes in the nose and sinus cavities; changes that may indicate underlying infection.

To complete this nasal examination, your doctor may order a special x-ray of the sinuses called *computerized tomography* (CT scan). In many cases, conventional x-rays may not show any evidence of sinus disease, whereas the CT scan provides finely detailed images of each sinus, from the frontal sinus in the forehead back to those at the base of the skull. A *radiologist* (physician specialized in x-ray diagnosis) usually interprets the CT scan images, working in collaboration with your doctor.

## Other Checkpoints

Physicians have come to understand the close association between sleep apnea and chronic lung disease. Many snorers are heavyset, overweight individuals and are also heavy smokers. Their impaired lung function may aggravate a mild case of apnea. Therefore, lung studies known as *pulmonary function tests*, may be recommended if you smoke and your medical/sleep history indicates a strong likelihood of sleep apnea.

The examination should also include an accurate assessment of your cardiovascular system. It is customary to record your blood pressure, taken while standing and supine, as well as to order an *electrocardiogram* (EKG). Your examining physician may also recommend an effort EKG, known as a *treadmill test.*

Although not routinely performed, measurements may be made between fixed bony points on the skull, taken from your x-rays. This test, called *cephalometry*, is now done in some university hospitals and sleep research facilities. Cephalometry attempts to correlate the relationship between anatomical structures in a person's head and the site of any upper airway obstruction. These measurements may help determine sources of existing obstruction, as well as aiding the physician in selecting appropriate medical or surgical procedures for a patient.

Your initial examination may provide your physician with the information needed to determine an effective treatment for your snoring. However, if sleep apnea is suspected and you need further investigation of your sleep habits, your doctor will usually recommend an overnight sleep study. You will be pleased to learn that although the equipment used in this sleep test is quite complex, the evaluation process is completely painless.

In fact, you'll be able to snooze right through it!

# Chapter 6

# An Overnight Sleep Test:

## You'll Snooze Right Through It

Two decades ago, only a small number of medical researchers were interested in sleep disorders; specialized facilities to study and treat patients suffering from these problems were scarce. This situation changed dramatically in the mid-1970's as more patients sought help for disorders associated with sleep. In 1987, the American Sleep Disorders Association was established to set standards, providing both certification and guidance for these rapidly emerging sleep disorders centers and their staffs.

Today, people with severe snoring problems can go to any of a number of knowledgeable physicians and sophisticated sleep disorders centers in all parts of the country, and, in fact, throughout the world. These facilities follow established standards, as do the three groups of professionals involved: Physicians associated with sleep disorders clinics; scientists doing basic sleep research; and technicians skilled in the administration of sleep testing.

If you or your partner are suspected of having sleep apnea and an overnight sleep study is recommended, you will no doubt have a number of preliminary questions about sleep testing in general and your own study in particular. I will take you through a typical night in a sleep disorders clinic so you can see exactly how such a test is conducted. But first, let's discuss some of the preliminary concerns you may have.

Here are some of the questions patients most often ask. They will, I believe, include most of your own:

♦ What is a sleep disorders center?

♦ Should I have a sleep test before seeing a physician?

♦ When is a sleep study recommended for a snorer?

♦ When is a sleep study *not* recommended for a snorer?

♦ Must a sleep disorders center be accredited?

♦ What are the costs, and which of them will my medical insurance cover?

♦ Is a sleep study recommended for a snoring child or for one suspected of sleep apnea?

Let's consider each of these questions more closely:

**What is a sleep disorders center?**
Usually housed within a hospital or medical center, a sleep disorders center—or sleep laboratory—is a diagnostic and short-term outpatient treatment facility, established to study some or all of the following:

♦ Difficulty in falling asleep.

♦ Difficulty in staying asleep, due, for example, to sleep-related breathing disorders.

♦ Abnormal behaviors during sleep (called *parasomnias*), such as sleepwalking, nightmares and night terrors.

+ Medical disorders associated with sleep, not occurring during waking hours, including abnormal movements during sleep, such as the *restless legs syndrome.*

+ The success and effectiveness of various medical and surgical treatments for any of the above disorders.

As a facility in a hospital or medical center, a sleep disorders center is supervised by medical specialists drawn from such disciplines as pulmonary medicine, neurology, psychiatry and psychology. In addition, the center's supervisory staff includes an *accredited polysomnographer* (sleep study specialist) whose responsibility is to train technicians, oversee data gathering, supervise the various tests, and provide reports on patients who are studied. The sleep center is staffed by technicians trained in gathering reliable sleep data. Consultants—specialists in ear, nose and throat (otolaryngologists), internal medicine and cardiology— often complement this team.

**Should I have a sleep test before seeing a physician?**
No, you will not be permitted to do so. Because a sleep disorders center is part of a medical facility, an overnight sleep study is considered a medical evaluation, therefore requiring a physician's referral.

**When is a sleep study recommended for a snorer?**

+ If you snore loudly enough to consistently disrupt the well-being of your bedroom partner, and especially if any surgery is contemplated, your physician may order this test to exclude sleep apnea.

+ If your initial sleep history and physical evaluation reveals any suspicion of sleep apnea.

+ If you suffer from excessive tiredness during waking hours and your physician suspects some underlying associated sleep disorder.

Most people seek medical help for their snoring because it *has* become disruptive. That's why an overnight stay at a sleep disorders center is frequently recommended for many patients with severe snoring or other sleep disorders as a follow-up to your doctor's preliminary findings.

**When is a sleep study *not* recommended for a snorer?**
If you are a socially-disruptive snorer without any of the symptoms commonly associated with sleep apnea, you may be advised to lose weight, exercise or modify any medications you are taking before requiring an overnight sleep study. In other words, a sleep study is generally not recommended in an otherwise healthy snorer. However, snoring is often the cardinal symptom alerting your doctor to the possibility of underlying sleep apnea. Your sleep history will therefore dictate, to a large extent, the need for this test.

**Must a sleep disorders center be accredited?**
Accreditation of any sleep disorders center refers to the broad range of diagnostic capabilities that a facility can offer. This identifies such a center as having the capacity to study a full spectrum of sleep disorders, such as narcolepsy, nighttime seizures, insomnia, nightmares, bed-wetting, sleepwalking and impotence, as well as ensuring good medical standards of testing and reporting.

Unlike studying some of these more complex disorders, monitoring snoring and testing for sleep apnea are fairly straightforward procedures. Any established sleep disorders center—accredited or nonaccredited—should be able to do it. What *is* important is that the testing be carefully done by trained personnel, and that the results represent a true and accurate evaluation of the problem.

However, your medical insurance carrier may consider

accreditation of any sleep disorders center a factor in deciding whether to cover the cost of your tests.

**What are the costs, and which of them will my medical insurance cover?**

In the current climate of managed health care, formal authorization from your insurance company is now usually required before any sleep studies are done. However, as the medical profession becomes more familiar with sleep disorders in general, medical insurances appear more amenable to recognize these issues and provide appropriate coverage.

Your medical insurance will probably cover the cost of the following:

♦ Your initial office evaluation, including sleep history and physical examination.

♦ Additional office tests, such as x-rays, *electro-cardiogram* (EKG) and blood tests.

♦ Overnight sleep testing.

Medical costs vary from county to county and from state to state, but the following represents the broad range of current charges:

♦ Complete *polysomnography* (all night sleep evaluation): $1000 to $1500.

♦ Unattended sleep monitoring: $700 to $1000.

Some insurance companies hesitate to cover testing for snoring alone, but will usually do so on the strength of a physician's opinion that the snoring might be one symptom of an underlying sleep-related breathing disorder.

**Is a sleep study recommended for a snoring child or for one suspected of sleep apnea?**

Usually not. Your pediatrician, family practitioner or ear,

nose and throat specialist can usually identify the specific site of obstruction in such a child's airway. This permits appropriate (and usually successful) treatment, rather than having to put any child through an expensive and somewhat frightening test experience.

I hope these answers address some of your concerns. When questions are asked, everyone benefits. Becoming actively involved in your own medical care is invaluable for you and your treating physicians. We must ask questions at every step along the way so that we can develop complete trust in each other. This book attempts to provide the information you need in order to ask the right questions.

## An Overnight Sleep Study

Your doctor has reviewed your sleep history and clinical findings with you and has recommended an overnight sleep study. What should you expect when this is done?

An overnight sleep test is unlike most other medical evaluations. For one thing, you can sleep right through it! Also, there are no injections, anesthetics or incisions, and there is no pain or discomfort. All you need to do is sleep in your natural way.

When your appointment with a sleep disorders center is made, you will be asked to come in a few hours before your usual bedtime. Ordinarily, you will have received a questionnaire and instructions concerning what you should bring with you (pajamas, toothbrush, robe, customary medications and usual reading material).

You will see that the sleep center's questionnaire contains many of the questions asked in your physician's preliminary evaluation. This redundancy is not due to a lack of communication between your physician and the center; it's just that the sleep center wants to have your medical information on its standard forms.

At the center, a member of the staff, usually the sleep center technician, will greet you and take you to your room—a cross between a hotel room and a hospital room. There, the technician will explain the nature of the test, tell you what to expect, show you what will be done and demonstrate the equipment to be used. Then he or she will attach the monitoring devices to your body.

You will learn that the *polysomnogram* (sleep evaluation data) is recorded on a *polysomnograph* and will be interpreted by a physician, usually a *certified clinical polysomnographer.* The sophisticated equipment used will monitor your brain waves, heart rhythms, breathing patterns, muscle tone, blood oxygen levels and body movements throughout the duration of your sleep test.

After you change into your nightclothes, the technician attaches the monitoring equipment to your face, head and body, using a special paste to ensure a firm seal for the electrodes. The wires from these monitoring sensors are plugged into a wall-jack in your room, transmitting information through a central line to a polysomnograph machine in an adjacent room—where your sleep patterns can be observed unobtrusively by the technician.

This monitoring equipment may cause anxiety in some people. To dispel any apprehensions it might provoke, let's take a closer look at the various sensors and explain their purpose:

### Measuring your breathing effort
Because this test helps decide whether you hold your breath during sleep, your breathing efforts are carefully measured by sensors attached to broad elastic bands, called *strain gauges.* These sensors, which fit snugly around your chest and abdomen, detect and record the amplitude of each breath.

Breathing normally, your chest expands with each breath, producing an even flow of air through your nose and mouth. With sleep apnea, however, air flow through your upper air passages is blocked, despite efforts by your chest muscles to continue breathing.

**Measuring your airflow**

The sleep technician will attach temperature-sensitive sensors to your upper lip. Known as *thermistors*, these devices record the minute amount of heating or cooling of air flowing in or out of your nose and mouth as you breathe.

When you hold your breath, however, there is no detectable temperature change. This component of your sleep test, read in conjunction with your breathing efforts, helps distinguish between central and obstructive sleep apnea.

**Measuring your oxygen levels**

A device called an *oximeter* is placed over your fingertip

(like a band-aid), or secured to your ear lobe with a little clip. This oximeter accurately records levels of oxygen by measuring the color of blood flowing through your skin. Under normal healthy circumstances, your blood is highly saturated with oxygen. When you hold your breath, however, such as occurs in sleep apnea, the blood oxygen rapidly becomes depleted.

This lowering of your oxygen level, known as *oxygen desaturation*, is a critical measure in determining the severity of sleep apnea.

### Measuring your heart rate

Electrodes are secured onto your chest to measure and record your heart rate and rhythm. This component of your sleep test is called an *electrocardiogram* (EKG).

Prolonged breath-holding during sleep can affect your heart, increasing or decreasing your pulse rate. In addition, sleep apnea, as we have learned, can be directly responsible for serious abnormalities of heart rhythm, some of which may be potentially fatal.

### Measuring your eye movements

The sleep center technician will secure electrodes near the corners of your eyes to record eye movements.

Known as *electro-oculograms* (EOG), these recordings capture the rapid eye movements (REM) we described in an earlier chapter as being associated with the deepest levels of sleep and with dreaming. This aspect of the test, therefore, helps your physician distinguish between your REM and non-REM sleep phases, correlating this with other recorded sleep data.

### Measuring your brain waves

Our brain constantly produces weak electrical signals. When amplified, these signals can be recorded onto a permanent record called an *electroencephalogram* (EEG).

Brain wave activity varies with wakefulness, sleep and dreaming. Your EEG, therefore, is a valuable guide for correlating any sleep apnea with different levels of sleep.

A technician attaches electrodes to your scalp, usually applying a special paste before gluing them onto head-positions corresponding with areas of your brain.

Don't worry, your hair won't be shaved. A shower and shampoo after this test will easily get rid of the glue and electrode paste.

### Measuring your body position and movements

In some sleep centers, additional sensors are introduced to record leg movements as well as changes in body position.

Just as some people snore only on their backs, sleep apnea may similarly be related to body positions. Additionally, restless leg movements may signify the typically disturbed sleep of sleep apnea, or may suggest the presence of some other sleep-related medical condition.

### Measuring your muscle tone

Electrodes are fixed to your chin to measure muscle tone. Known as *electromyography* (EMG), these sensors record variations in the tension or relaxation of your muscles, associated with different phases of sleep.

These various sensing devices continuously record your physical and physiological patterns during your overnight sleep study. Though they may differ in number, appearance and body placement from one sleep disorders center to another, they will be functionally identical, monitoring the fundamental sleep behavior needing to be studied in an effort to bring your disruptive nights to an end.

Although this monitoring equipment is somewhat confining, you will be able to turn over in bed and assume your natural sleeping position. You will be asked to use the bathroom before the sensors are attached, but if you have

# A Fully Operational Sleep Disorders Center

An accredited facility will provide the following:

1. Two or more separate sleeping rooms, equipped with two-way intercoms.

2. Each room equipped with polysomnograph machines to record the specific functions being monitored on 8 to 14 channels.

3. An accurate method for all-night monitoring of arterial blood oxygen, such as a transcutaneous ear oximeter (a device attached to your ear which measures blood-oxygen ratios through the skin).

4. One full-time technician who conducts polysomnography (sleep recording) during the night.

5. One full-time daytime technician who prepares for the nightly studies, scores records and conducts daytime testing.

6. An office to process and store laboratory data.

7. A clinical coordinator to facilitate patient referrals for associated studies such as pulmonary function, cardiac studies and electroencephalo-grams.

8. An accredited clinical polysomnographer (a medically qualified sleep evaluator who may be an M.D. or a Ph.D.).

9. A full-time physician with expertise in sleep physiology to assure continuity of medical care in the evaluation of sleep disorders patients.

10. Good working relations with associated clinical services of cardiology, neurology, otolaryngology, pediatrics, psychiatry, pulmonary medicine and urology.

11. In-hospital emergency code coverage whenever sleep patients are monitored.

to answer nature's call during the actual test, the technician will provide a bedpan.


## Your Sleep Center Technician

Before we leave the sleep center, let's take a closer look at your sleep technician—the person who diligently watches while you sleep.

Your overnight sleep study is supervised by a technician, whose special training ensures that these tests are conducted safely, comfortably and accurately.

The American Sleep Disorders Association has developed strict guidelines for the education and training of sleep technicians. The accuracy of any sleep test depends largely on the ability of your technician to prepare the equipment, attach the sensors carefully and supervise the recordings according to designated standards.

The sleep technician's special training, therefore, is of paramount importance to obtain the most accurate and reliable information from your sleep test.

In most sleep centers, at least one member of the staff will be a *Registered Polysomnographic Technologist*, a credential earned by completing supervised training as well as a written test.


## Listening to Learn More

In addition to the sensors I have described, you will notice that there is a microphone in the room. This allows the technician to listen to your breathing and record the degree of your snoring. It also allows you to communicate with the technician, should you need anything during the night.

There will probably be a TV/video camera and a one-way mirror in your room for further observation. This camera is usually placed on the opposite side of the bed from the mirror, allowing the technician to observe your behavior continually, confirming that sensors remain attached, should you turn over in your sleep.

Some sleep disorders centers—not all—make an audiotape of your snoring, or an audiovisual tape of the complete sleep sample. Because snoring is a cardinal symptom of nocturnal upper airway obstruction, it is important that the intensity of your snoring (loudness, frequency and duration) be accurately studied. The result is better patient evaluation, improved treatment planning and more accurate assessment of the success of treatment methods. It also provides objective documentation for your physician.

The technique for measuring and recording the sounds of snoring is known as *sleep sonography*. Typically, a microphone is placed near the snorer's head; the electrical signal is fed into a noise analyzer and tape-recorder. This analyzer classifies signals from the microphone, transferring data to a computer for display and storage, in both graphic and tabular form.

When you are ready to go to sleep, the technician turns off the lights (remember, you can't leave the bed) and watches brain waves, recorded on the polysomnograph, noting the exact time sleep occurs. Throughout the night, sensors send signals to the polysomnograph; these signals are converted into electrical impulses, appearing as wavy lines on the continuous sheets of paper fed into the machine. During a single night's sleep recording, more than one-half mile of paper may be covered with squiggles and waves. In recent years, however, sleep recordings are captured on computer disks, more convenient for both storage and interpretation.

In the morning, you will be asked questions about how

you slept, including estimates of how long it took you to fall asleep, how often you awakened, and how this night compared with a normal night's rest at home. The purpose of these questions is to correlate the recorded information with your own impression of the experience.

The sleep center technician helps you remove any electrode paste from your scalp and body. Then, after a shower and a welcome cup of coffee, you will be on your way, early enough to be on time for work.

At the conclusion of your sleep test, data from the polysomnograph is processed by a computer, calculating the time it took you to fall asleep, the duration of each sleep stage, awakenings, breathing patterns, apneic episodes, changes in heart rate and final awakening. A medical specialist, associated with the sleep center, correlates this information in a report to the referring physician.

Before going on to review a typical sleep test report with you, I should mention that in rare instances a sleep test may have to be repeated, for the following reasons:

♦ You were unable to sleep at all (which rarely occurs).

♦ You and your physician feel that the test is not a truly representative sleep sample. (You slept poorly, had nightmares, touches of insomnia or a fitful sleep.)

♦ You slept quietly through the night and never snored, despite a history of severe snoring which led to the test in the first place.

♦ There were technical problems (for example, a dislodged sensor went unnoticed) preventing a complete and accurate test recording.

## A Sleep Study Report

To illustrate a typical sleep evaluation, we will review the case report of a patient I'll call Bill. He consulted with me because of severe nighttime snoring in all body positions. His wife had become concerned with his irregular breathing and restless sleep behavior. On questioning, Bill admitted to some daytime drowsiness, occasionally dozing off in church or at the movies. Physical examination showed a man in good health, although somewhat overweight. A nose and throat examination revealed no abnormality other than slight enlargement of his tonsils. Because of his eroding quality of sleep and daytime fatigue, I recommended that Bill undergo an overnight sleep study. The following report came to me from the sleep center:

> This 48-year-old male was referred because of loud, habitual snoring throughout the night, in all positions, irregular breathing during sleep and episodes of suspected apnea. He experiences some degree of daytime drowsiness.
>
> An overnight sleep study was performed in our sleep center, and the patient was studied in the usual manner with bipolar electroencephalograph leads. Nasal and oral thermistors, thoracic and abdominal strain gauges were applied. An earlobe oximeter was attached. This study is of good technical quality. The patient had sufficient amounts of REM sleep for interpretation.
>
> The patient commenced sleeping without difficulty and was observed to snore throughout the entire sleep sample. He slept on his back for most of the study, turning occasionally onto his left side. Total sleep time was 362 minutes. During this sample, 180 respiratory disturbances (apneas and hypopneas) were observed and recorded. The respiratory disturbance index was calculated as 30. These episodes varied in duration from 14 to 41 seconds,

with an average of 26 seconds. During the longest
apneas, his pulse rate fell to below 50 beats per
minute, and blood oxygen saturation levels dropped
to 76 percent.

Comment: This patient is a severe snorer with
significant obstructive sleep apnea. The apneas are
associated with marked reduction in blood oxygen
saturation levels as well as bradycardic episodes
(slowing of the heart rate).

To understand the significance of this report, we need
to familiarize ourselves with some of the terminology used
by physicians in sleep disorders centers.

The basic measure used to express the severity of any
patient's sleep apnea is known as the *apnea index*. This
measurement is determined by calculating the number of
apneas recorded during each hour of sleep. If, for example,
you had 25 apneas during each hour of a 6-hour sleep test
(a total of 150 apneas), this would yield an apnea index of
25.

However, breathing interruptions recorded during overnight sleep studies frequently show very shallow breaths
(called hypopneas) together with epochs of completely
obstructed breathing. Formerly, these hypopneas would
not have been included in the apnea index. Today, however, because any shallow, ineffectual hypopnea is essentially the same as a complete breath-holding episode (apnea), we now combine the number of recorded apneas together with hypopneas. This composite number is referred
to as the *respiratory disturbance index* (RDI).

Say, for example, your sleep test showed 25 apneas and
10 hypopneas during each hour of sleep, your respiratory
disturbance index would be 35. The RDI therefore, ex-
presses the total number of recorded breathing interrup-

tions, representing a more accurate measure of your sleep apnea.

Another indicator of a patient's sleep apnea is the level to which their blood oxygen falls during a sleep test. In other words, the degree of oxygen desaturation reflects both the frequency and the duration of the repeated apneas.

Under normal circumstances, our blood is 95 percent or more saturated with oxygen. In people with sleep apnea, this number will often fall below 90 percent. How-

## Measuring the Severity of Obstructive Sleep Apnea

| Sleep Apnea | Snoring | Sleepiness | Apnea Index | Blood Oxygen Desaturation (percent) | Heart Rate and Rhythm Changes |
|---|---|---|---|---|---|
| Mild | Yes | Intermittent | 11-30 | Above 75 | No |
| Moderate | Yes | Constant | 30 or more | 50-74 | No |
| Severe | Yes | Debilitating | 30 or more | Below 50 | Yes |

ever, even lower oxygen desaturation is considered dangerous, because of the potentially harmful effects on our heart and brain.

Although not universally accepted, one useful classification of the severity of sleep apnea, developed at Stanford University School of Medicine Sleep Disorders Center, is shown in the accompanying table.

Here's how I interpreted the sleep lab report to Bill: "Based on your constant loud snoring, your daytime sleepiness, apneic episodes, oxygen desaturation levels and changes in your heart rate recorded during your sleep study, I would say that you are a severe snorer who is suffering from a moderate degree of obstructive sleep apnea."

What Bill's sleep history, his daytime behavior, and his wife's observations had suggested, the sleep center's data had accurately confirmed. We were then able to consider appropriate corrective measures.

## Ambulatory or Unattended Sleep Monitoring

Now I want to discuss a more informal but nonetheless accurate sleep evaluation procedure, playing an increasingly prominent role in the diagnosis and treatment of sleep-related breathing disorders. This test is conveniently administered at home in the privacy of your bedroom. Because a technician is not present while you sleep, this test is called an *unattended sleep study*.

While sleep disorders centers are rapidly multiplying (some authorities estimate that in the United States alone they number around 5,000), they aren't yet available in all parts of the country and might never be. But not everyone suspected of sleep apnea needs to go to one. Several years ago, portable monitoring devices were developed, enabling patients to obtain nighttime sleep studies at home. Known as an *ambulatory monitoring system*, this is a microcomputer designed for continuous analysis of information from multiple physiological sensors. This small, lightweight system is fitted and adjusted at your home by a technician, who returns to collect the equipment in the morning. The data are then collated and a report is generated for your physician.

Worn on a belt or placed next to the bed, this ambulatory monitoring system records the following data:

- Blood oxygen saturation levels.
- Nasal air flow.
- Thoracic and abdominal expansion (respiratory efforts).
- Heart rate and abnormal heart rhythm.
- Body movements.

Recent advances in this technology allow for recording EOG (for eye movement), EEG (for REM and non-REM sleep differentiation) and EMG (for recording muscle tone).

Although these home-use devices cannot substitute for all the comprehensive testing you can get in a hospital-based sleep center, sleep researchers acknowledge that ambulatory monitoring now plays an increasingly valuable role in the study of sleep-related breathing disorders. When your physician suspects a mild or moderate degree of apnea, and by medical history can exclude other sleep-related disorders, the ambulatory monitoring system may be a useful and less expensive way to document and measure your apnea. Some patients feel that because this test is done right in their own bedroom, it reflects a more natural, representative sample of their sleep habits.

Because unattended monitoring is essentially a simpler test, requiring less equipment with fewer personnel, it is less expensive than a sleep center test. This is certainly a consideration. Many insurance companies provide coverage for these home-based tests, but you should determine this before having the study.

At present, the following concerns exist regarding the use of unattended monitoring systems:

- This study is less complete than that produced by a traditional sleep disorders center.
- Because no formal accreditation or quality-control

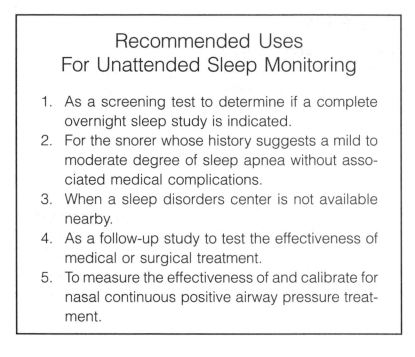

# Recommended Uses
# For Unattended Sleep Monitoring

1.  As a screening test to determine if a complete overnight sleep study is indicated.
2.  For the snorer whose history suggests a mild to moderate degree of sleep apnea without associated medical complications.
3.  When a sleep disorders center is not available nearby.
4.  As a follow-up study to test the effectiveness of medical or surgical treatment.
5.  To measure the effectiveness of and calibrate for nasal continuous positive airway pressure treatment.

exists for unattended sleep study programs, there may be variations in the accuracy of these tests.

♦ The absence of a technical observer during the test may detract from its accuracy—for example, a sensor may become dislodged during sleep.

♦ Medically trained personnel are not at hand in the event of an emergency such as cardiac arrest during sleep. This is one reason why high risk patients are not recommended for home-study monitoring.

The decision to perform any test is ultimately made by your physician. Having information about the various methods available for evaluating snoring and sleep apnea, however, puts you in a better position to discuss the pros and cons of these tests with your doctor.

## It's a SNAP

Home monitoring systems for snoring and sleep apnea have been on the market for the past 15 or 16 years. Some of these devices have been criticized by sleep specialists for providing results that are either incomplete or inaccurate.

A new home system, called *SNAP*™, monitors snoring and sleep apnea by recording and analyzing breathing sounds during sleep. Employing a small microphone attached to the face, near the nose and mouth, breathing sounds are captured on tape then sent to a laboratory for acoustic analysis. Results of recordings with this *SNAP* system compared favorably in accuracy with complete polysomnography for the detection of sleep apnea.

The manufacturers of this device claim that acoustic analysis can pinpoint the maximal site of snoring in the upper airway, making the choice of an invasive procedure more accurate. In addition, *SNAP* can also be utilized for CPAP titration, a function especially useful in smaller, outlying communities where access to a sleep disorders center is difficult or inconvenient.

Finally, the *SNAP* system can be used to record sleep disordered breathing in children (above the age of 3) for both clinical and research purposes. The ease with which a recording cannula can be applied to a child, while sleeping, permits accurate recordings. Conversely, polysomnography with its array of multiple electrodes and monitoring devices, in a strange environment, obviously represents a stressful and daunting experience to any young child.

# Tests for Hypersomnolence

## (Excessive Daytime Sleepiness)

The sleep disorders center also plays a vital role in diagnosing patients who suffer from excessive daytime sleepiness (EDS), which we call *hypersomnolence*. We know that hypersomnolence is a frequent by-product of sleep apnea and must be distinguished from other neurological conditions with similar symptoms, such as narcolepsy (an irresistible urge to fall asleep during the day).

If you have a history of daytime sleepiness and fatigue (without snoring), you are likely to be scheduled for a *Multiple Sleep Latency Test* in addition to an overnight sleep study. The standard sleep monitoring described in this chapter is used to measure the time taken to get back to sleep after being awakened. The patient is allowed to take four or five short naps at approximately two-hour intervals during the day. He is monitored until stage 1 or 2 NREM sleep is reached or until 20 minutes have elapsed. He is then awakened, recording the time required to resume sleeping. The report contains the average sleep latency (the time taken to resume sleeping) as well as the number of REM periods during sleep.

This "nap test" allows the treating physician to grade the degree of hypersomnolence. Here is how physicians classify excessive daytime sleepiness (EDS):

**Mild EDS:** Patient can stay awake while motivated by work or social activities, but tends to become drowsy when external stimuli are removed.

**Moderate EDS:** Patient falls asleep while inactive or when at work, with increasing social and economic side effects as a result. Driving is a concern for such a patient.

**Severe EDS:** Patient cannot stay awake during the day, even when motivated or stimulated. Such a patient is in constant danger of having industrial or automobile accidents.

After you spend a night in the sleep disorders center, or after an unattended study, your doctor will be able to determine whether your snoring is associated with sleep apnea, and how severe it is.

## The Epworth Sleepiness Scale

While the Multiple Sleep Latency Test is reliable as an accurate measure of daytime sleepiness, it is cumbersome, time-consuming and expensive to perform. As a result, a questionnaire known as the Epworth Sleepiness Scale has been designed to measure daytime sleepiness in a simple, economic yet standardized way.

This concept was developed by sleep researchers in Australia, derived from observing the nature and occurrence of daytime sleep and sleepiness. Some people who suffer from excess daytime sleepiness are able to keep themselves busy, choosing not to lie down and rest or relax during the day, purposely avoiding the temptation to fall asleep. Others who may not be very sleepy, choose to sleep during the day out of sheer boredom or inactivity. By contrast, sleepy people often describe their tendency to doze off while engaged in activities requiring low levels of stimulation, such as watching a movie or television.

The Epworth Sleepiness Scale is therefore based on questions referring to eight situations, some of which are known to promote sleepiness, others less so. Subjects are asked to rate on a scale of 0 to 3 their likelihood of falling asleep in a variety of situations based on their usual way of life. This test makes a distinction between dozing off and simply feeling tired.

The numbers selected for the eight situations described in the questionnaire are added together, giving a score for each subject between 0 and 24. A score of less than 8 is considered normal; 8 to 11 is borderline abnormal; 11 to

# The Epworth Sleepiness Scale

Name: _____

Date: _____

Age: _____

This questionnaire addresses your tendency to doze off or fall asleep in the following situations, in contrast to merely feeling tired. Use the following scale to describe the most appropriate number for each situation:

> 0 = would never doze
> 1 = slight chance of dozing
> 2 = moderate chance of dozing
> 3 = high chance of dozing

| Chance of Dozing | Situation |
| --- | --- |
| _____ | Sitting and reading |
| _____ | Watching TV |
| _____ | Sitting, inactive in a public place (e.g., a movie or a meeting) |
| _____ | As a car passenger for at least an hour |
| _____ | Lying down to rest in the afternoon when circumstances permit |
| _____ | Sitting and talking with someone |
| _____ | Sitting quietly after a lunch without alcohol |
| _____ | Driving a car, while stopped for a few minutes in traffic |

16 represents moderate sleepiness and more than 16, severe sleepiness. The scores developed by applying this questionnaire compare very favorably with more sophisticated, expensive tests as a reliable measure of any individual's general level of daytime sleepiness. As a result, the Epworth Sleepiness Scale is now being applied in sleep disorder centers throughout the world.

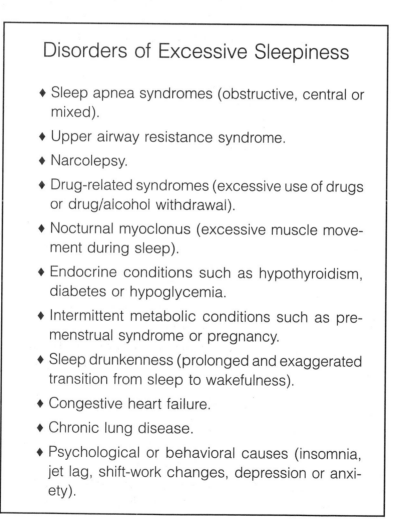

## Disorders of Excessive Sleepiness

♦ Sleep apnea syndromes (obstructive, central or mixed).

♦ Upper airway resistance syndrome.

♦ Narcolepsy.

♦ Drug-related syndromes (excessive use of drugs or drug/alcohol withdrawal).

♦ Nocturnal myoclonus (excessive muscle movement during sleep).

♦ Endocrine conditions such as hypothyroidism, diabetes or hypoglycemia.

♦ Intermittent metabolic conditions such as premenstrual syndrome or pregnancy.

♦ Sleep drunkenness (prolonged and exaggerated transition from sleep to wakefulness).

♦ Congestive heart failure.

♦ Chronic lung disease.

♦ Psychological or behavioral causes (insomnia, jet lag, shift-work changes, depression or anxiety).

By now, your physician should have sufficient information to decide on appropriate treatment for your snoring and/or sleep apnea. However, before considering current methods of therapy offering improvement or cure, I want to take a step back in time and examine some of the weird and wonderful devices invented by would-be snore-stoppers down the ages.

# Chapter 7

# Snoring: The Mother of Invention

S noring rattles the rafters in so many households that the challenge to silence it has proven irresistible to inventors over many years. They have examined, poked, prodded and analyzed this problem in search of a cure—any cure—that would bring nighttime silence to their bedrooms and overnight fame to themselves.

Without any doubt, posterity would enshrine the inventor of a true snore-stopper. In fact, an article in a national health magazine once suggested that the Nobel committee should seriously consider awarding their peace prize to the person perfecting a snoring cure!

Unfortunately, some would-be laureates have stumbled on their way to Stockholm. Consider this letter one inventor wrote to the *Ladies' Home Journal* in 1915:

> Many years ago, I was one of those violent, house-shaking snorers, producing sounds like the rumbles

> of Mt. Etna. Suddenly a plan occurred to me, which,
> when adopted, effected a cure. Many years have
> elapsed without any more snoring. My only regret is
> that I have forgotten the plan!

A numbing variety of antisnoring devices have appeared on the market, often listed in mail-order catalogs. Many of these products have been enthusiastically promoted and advertised, enjoying a season or two of popularity before disappearing from view. And as farfetched as many of these gadgets may appear, the concepts that inspired them are reasonably sound. All the inventors seem to have had some understanding of the mechanics of snoring. This is evident from the fact that their devices can be classified into the following categories:

- ♦ Appliances to keep the snorer off his back.
- ♦ Devices to keep the mouth closed and to prevent the tongue from falling backward.
- ♦ Contrivances to extend the neck.
- ♦ Instruments to startle the snorer with a shock or physical stimulus.

## Peculiar Patents That Seek to Cure

Over 300 of these antisnoring devices are listed in the gazettes of the U.S. Government Office of Patents. Perhaps, like so many other inventions, they were born out of necessity, or even desperation. You would think that the disgruntled female snoree, prompted by all those sleepless nights she was forced to endure, would be the inventor. But no, virtually all of these aspiring snore-scientists were male.

It has long been observed that snoring is aggravated when the sleeper lies on his back. Ingenious minds eventually recognized that such snoring could be controlled by keeping the snorer on his side. As far back as the Revolutionary War, it was customary to sew a small cannonball into a back-pocket on a soldier's uniform to keep him from sleeping on his back and awakening his comrades-in-arms.

A turn-of-the-century version of this snore-ball technique was developed by Leonidas Wilson in 1900. A leather brace was wrapped around the snorer's upper body, holding a multipronged object between his shoulder blades—guaranteeing, I've no doubt, extreme discomfort if he should ever turn onto his back as he slept.

A modern version of this antisnoring technique is to sew a pocket on the back of a pajama top or T-shirt and put a tennis ball or golf ball into it. Obviously, the sleeper experiences severe discomfort if he turns over onto his back, so he attempts to find a more comfortable position, presumably ending his snoring in the process. Some sleepers, after several months of this conditioning technique, become so used to lying on their side that they can dispense with the snore-ball and sleep comfortably, snore-free.

 Some motion-restraining devices are truly complex and ambitious, resembling a type of straitjacket rigidly holding the snorer in one position, on his side. Presumably,

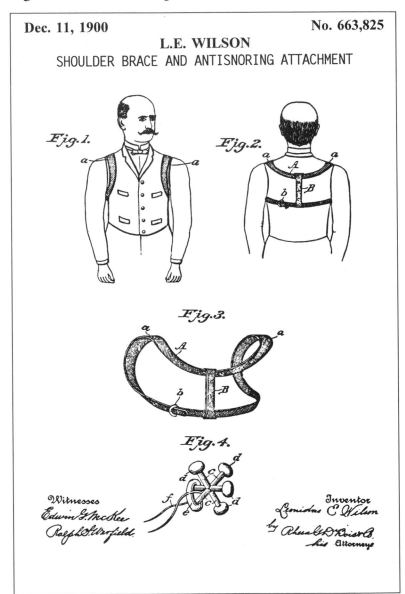

Dec. 11, 1900  No. 663,825

**L.E. WILSON**
SHOULDER BRACE AND ANTISNORING ATTACHMENT

Fig.1.

Fig.2.

Fig.3.

Fig.4.

Witnesses
Edwin G. McKee
Ralph S. Warfield.

Inventor
Leonidas E. Wilson
by Rhea &c. Boies &c.
his Attorneys

you would need the skills of Harry Houdini to escape the clutches of these snore-stoppers and even make it out of bed in the morning!

Many and varied inventions were created to restrict mouth breathing as a way to curb snoring. These prod-

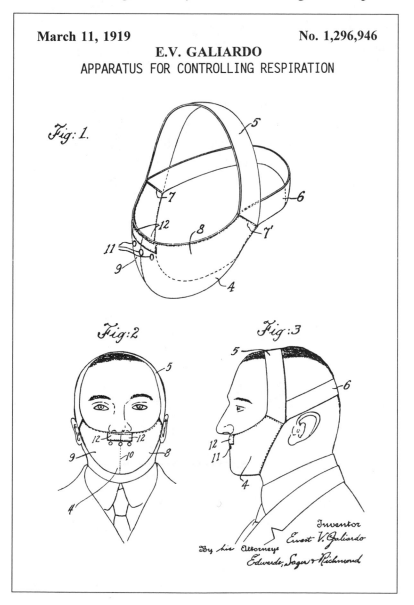

**March 11, 1919**                    **No. 1,296,946**

**E.V. GALIARDO**
APPARATUS FOR CONTROLLING RESPIRATION

ucts—called *mouth-dams*—follow the simple theory that if you breathe through your nose instead of your mouth, you won't snore.

In 1918, Ernest Galiardo developed and patented an elastic mask, fitting snugly over the sleeper's head, compressing his jaw so that his mouth stayed closed. Galiardo called his creation an *apparatus for controlling respiration*—which it surely must have done!

Ten years later, Richard Garvey filed a patent for his mouth-closing device. It contained a blade fitting between the snorer's lips, a guard to keep his mouth closed, and straps securing the entire contraption to the sleeper's ears.

George Foster's antisnoring gadget, patented in 1947, simply kept the mouth closed from dusk to dawn. A wonderful invention, no doubt, for snorers prone to talk in their sleep. And especially useful for wives with snoring husbands who voice too many opinions, Texan Walter G. Johnson's patent to correct mouth breathing, filed in 1922, soon shut them up. Good work, Wally!

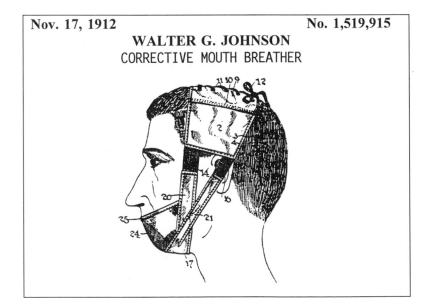

**Nov. 17, 1912**                              **No. 1,519,915**
### WALTER G. JOHNSON
CORRECTIVE MOUTH BREATHER

At last we come to a device invented by a woman. Elsa Leppich showed the world exactly how she felt about her husband's rumblings when she patented her antisnoring device in 1951, consisting of a tongue retainer and lip guard. History does not record the success of this apparatus or the fate of the Leppich marriage. We can only hope for their happiness.

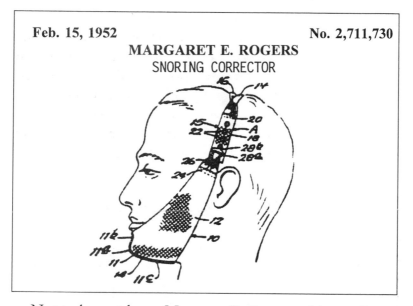

**Feb. 15, 1952**                                    **No. 2,711,730**

### MARGARET E. ROGERS
SNORING CORRECTOR

Not to be outdone, Margaret E. Rogers of Ames, Iowa, only one year later, battened down her hatches with a snoring-corrector. She claimed that her invention could overcome snoring without interfering with mouth-opening movements. I wonder what Mr. Rogers had to say about this? Or whether he could say anything at all?

## Chin Up Chaps!

Other inventors endeavored to keep the snorer's mouth shut with a bewildering variety of chin-straps and head-caps. Antisnoring devices in this class represent some of the earliest inventions.

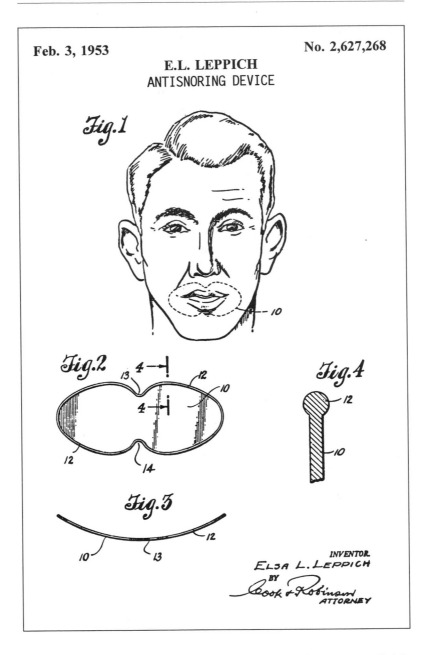

**E.L. LEPPICH**
ANTISNORING DEVICE

Fig.1

Fig.2    13   4    12   10    4    12   14

Fig.4   12   10

Fig.3    12   10   13

INVENTOR.
ELSA L. LEPPICH
BY
Cook & Robinson
ATTORNEY

Way back in 1893, Francis W. Pulford of Carson, Michigan, filed a patent for a chin-bandage which he called a *facial molding device*. Seven years later, Jacob S. Baughman of Burlington, Iowa, produced a head bandage which included a chin-sling with friction slides to facilitate movement. I suspect, from the appearance of this device, that movement for the sleeper was something of an impossible dream!

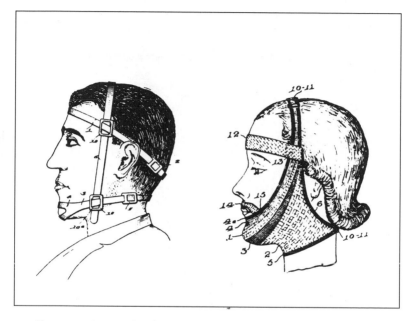

One patent which caught my attention while going through the files of old U.S. patent gazettes was an antimouth-breathing device, filed by John W. Rothenberger of Syracuse, Indiana, in 1919. I couldn't help but wonder whether a snorer would be able to close his eyes and get one moment's rest with this contraption in place.

I was also intrigued by the ingenuity of a mouth-restrainer, patented in 1948 by Cyrus Johnson. His invention offered the additional feature of keeping the upper airway clear by extending the sleeper's neck. Although I fear that Johnson's appliance might have given many a snorer a stiff neck, the principle of keeping the airway open by elevating the chin is well recognized in modern medical practice.

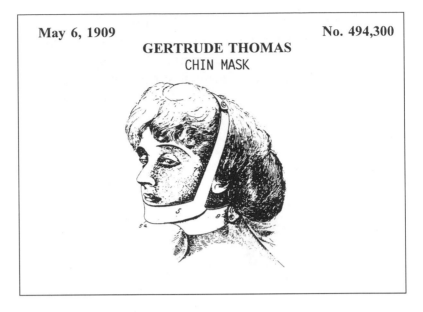

May 6, 1909                                    No. 494,300

**GERTRUDE THOMAS**
CHIN MASK

Johnson was actually anticipating an approach that was employed years later by Robert Elman, M.D., a St. Louis physician, in a clinical experiment reported in the 1961 *Journal of the American Medical Association:*

> A young patient wrote to me from his honeymoon, expressing fear that his marriage would fail because his snoring kept his bride awake so much that they were forced to occupy separate cabins. I had him examined and found no evidence of obstruction or disease in the nose or throat. Conventional treatment, such as making him sleep on his side and keeping his mouth closed, failed to bring relief and I therefore tried a new method. I remembered the obstructive breathing and snoring that frequently occurs during general anesthesia when the chin is allowed to drop; this is relieved immediately by extending the neck. Acting on this idea, I fitted the patient with a simple, easily applied and removed orthopedic collar, asking him to use it at night. He

was greatly pleased, for the device had eliminated his disability and for the first time his wife was able to get a good night's sleep. The patient subsequently discarded the collar and merely slept on his back with a small pillow at the nape of his neck. He is now happily married and has two children.

Turning his attention to a different source of the snoring, Henry Molow, a dentist in Brooklyn, New York, in 1953 developed a nasal device which he called "the Better Breathing Tube." Fitting into the nose, this tube was designed to prevent collapse of soft tissues on each side of the nasal opening. Testimonials from Dr. Molow's patients using this device indicate that they all stopped snoring.

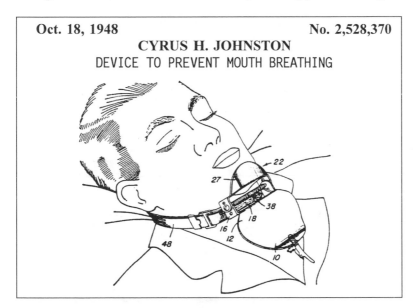

**Oct. 18, 1948**                                    **No. 2,528,370**
**CYRUS H. JOHNSTON**
DEVICE TO PREVENT MOUTH BREATHING

## Crime and Punishment

As we know, the cannonball or snore-ball method keeps the sleeper off his back through the principle of reward and punishment. The success of this approach has led to the invention of modern devices aimed at changing snorers' nightly behavior and conditioning them to become blissfully quiet sleepers.

In 1960, George Wilson of Groton, Connecticut was well on his way to a Nobel Peace Prize with his mouth-opening alarm, designed to kill at least two birds with one snore! If this gadget effectively curtailed both snoring *and* speaking, as George intended, the Wilson household must have been the quietest in Connecticut.

The Snore Stopper, currently sold by mail order, claims to eliminate snoring "effectively and inexpensively, without drugs or surgery." A microphone in this gadget picks up the sound of snoring, triggering a mechanism which gives the sleeper a mild electric shock, not quite severe enough to awaken him. But the Snore Stopper repeats the stimulus with each loud snore. The object is, of course, to condition the snorer by making him uncomfortable enough to change his behavior so he can enjoy a good night's rest without interruption.

One conditioning device, an electronic sound-detector which sets off a buzzer alarm in response to loud snor-

## THE SNORE STOPPER
### INSTRUCTION BOOKLET
**Please read this instruction booklet before using the Snore Stopper.**

ing, has a whimsical twist. The snorer has to get out of bed to deactivate the buzzer. The machine, however, provides a piece of candy as a reward.

A wonderful, though admittedly mischievous, Rube Goldberg antisnoring device is known, among inventors, as the "Snorgone 2000Z." As the blissful sleeper drifts deeper into unconsciousness, his body movements are monitored by a rumble-sensor, while a blast-resistant microphone picks up the intensifying din of his snoring. These readings continue as the snoring gets ever louder. At a critical point, the seismometer unleashes a series of snore-deterrents upon the hapless snorer:

- ♦ A flashlight suddenly shines into his eyes!
- ♦ A "sound-activated beak-tweeker" pinches him on the nose!
- ♦ A loudspeaker subjects him to the sound of his own ferocious snoring!
- ♦ A glass of cold water is tossed in his face!
- ♦ The snoring ceases . . . maybe!

Although the Snorgone 2000Z is clearly a tongue-in-cheek creation, some medical men were hard at work developing legitimate antisnore systems. Harvey Flack, M.D., of England, was one of them.

In 1960 Dr. Flack conducted experiments to determine what makes a snorer snore and which muscles, tissues and organs are involved. After firmly establishing these facts, Dr. Flack and his colleagues developed a series of exercises, which they hoped would provide the long-sought-after cure for snoring. But these investigators knew that their theory had to prove its value in practice. It had to be tested.

## Snore No More with Dr. Flack

Dr. Flack placed a notice in a British Medical Association magazine asking for snorers to volunteer for his project. This notice was headed, "Wanted Urgently—People Who Snore," and concluded with the promise: "There is at least an even chance that you will start the New Year with your snoring cured."

The response exceeded all expectations. Newspapers in Britain and countries all over the world reprinted the notices. Dr. Flack was deluged by letters. He stopped counting after the first 3,000—even though the letters continued to pour in. Ultimately, 250 volunteer snorers were selected, representing a cross-section of those whose jaws or tongues fell back during sleep or whose palates vibrated excessively. Dr. Flack and his medical team gave these volunteers a series of exercises to tighten and improve the tone of their throat, jaw, and tongue muscles. Each volunteer was instructed to perform a set of exercises nightly for the next two weeks:

♦ Hold something, such as a pencil, firmly between your teeth for 10 minutes after going to bed but before settling down to sleep. After several minutes your jaw muscles will ache, and this is to be expected.

◆ For 2 to 3 minutes, press your fingers firmly against your chin and hold your jaw steady against the pressure of your fingers.

◆ Press your tongue against your lower teeth for 3 to 4 minutes. If you have no teeth, hold a finger to your mouth and press your tongue against it.

When the study was completed, Dr. Flack found that the exercises had been effective in many cases; in fact, the majority of the volunteers happily reported that their snoring had been appreciably curbed. Even so, Dr. Flack was less optimistic.

"I am not hopeful about a cure for snoring," he said. "It is true to say that if people are otherwise healthy and are throat snorers, about half can be helped if they work at my exercises. But otherwise, it is unlikely that anyone will come up with anything dramatic or sensational."

"It comes to this: Snoring that threatens marriages or makes difficulties of that kind is in the province of the marriage counselor, not the doctor."

Dr. Flack, however, may have been too hard on himself. His exercises appear to be safe and may be worth trying, as they are designed to improve muscle tone in the tissues of the upper respiratory tract.

## Safety Tips Concerning "Cures"

Not all patented methods for the cure of snoring are safe, and if you are going to experiment with any of them I recommend the following cautions:

◆ The use of any device to prevent mouth breathing requires that the user's nose be clear. Nasal obstruction of any cause—from colds, allergies, or polyps—may require medical or surgical treatment before using one of these appliances.

◆ Any body-restraining device can produce stiff joints

and muscles as well as interfere with blood circulation.

♦ If you suspect that sleep apnea is associated with your snoring, seek medical advice rather than use over-the-counter "cures."

♦ Don't be fooled by expensive gadgets advertised as guaranteed cures in magazines and catalogs.

♦ Discuss any self-help advice or method with a physician to be sure it is reasonable for use in conjunction with your medical treatment.

By now, we've discussed the causes, effects and social fallout produced by snoring. You have learned about sleep apnea and its various medical sequelae.

You have also taken a Snore Score quiz to assess your own snoring. In the past few chapters, you have been introduced to sleep disorders specialists, primary care physicians and ear, nose and throat surgeons. We have taken you through a typical night in a sleep disorders center as well as describing a similar test done in the privacy of your home. You have also learned how to interpret the results of these sleep tests.

Finally, we've looked at some tried (but not trusted) remedies and nostrums. It is now time to consider some of the more up-to-date treatments for this age-old problem.

# Chapter 8

# Modern Medical and Surgical Treatment

## For Snoring and Sleep Apnea

Wouldn't it be wonderful if every snorer's companion could go down to the local drugstore, purchase a bottle of "antisnore," sprinkle a few drops over the beloved's bedtime snack, and be rewarded with a silent, snore-free night?

Unfortunately, there is no such miracle product. But that doesn't mean snoring cannot be effectively curtailed or even cured. In fact, snoring can be alleviated by a variety of methods, ranging from lifestyle changes to medical, mechanical and surgical treatments. The method appropriate for you depends, to a large extent, on your answers to the following questions:

♦ Is your snoring loud enough to regularly disturb your bedroom partner?

♦ Are you a socially disruptive snorer, in otherwise good

health, or do you have disturbed sleep and daytime tiredness? In other words, is there a possibility that you suffer from sleep apnea?

♦ If obstructive sleep apnea does accompany your snoring, where does the obstruction occur in your upper respiratory tract?

♦ If sleep apnea has been diagnosed during an overnight sleep study, how severe is it? What is your respiratory disturbance index and oxygen desaturation level? Has your sleep apnea progressed to the point of producing medical side-effects?

♦ Do you suffer from morning fatigue and excessive daytime sleepiness in relation to your sleep apnea? If so, to what degree?

## Lifestyle Changes

If questionnaires or evaluation proves that you do not have sleep apnea, then a few changes in your lifestyle and sleep habits might reduce or possibly eliminate your snoring.

Where and how you sleep can affect your snoring. So can what you eat and drink, and when. And if you are overweight, that might be at the core of your snoring problem. Check your lifestyle against some of these tips and cautions:

### Changing Your Sleep Habits

Changing your position during sleep is one possible answer to snoring, but not the only one. Consider these helpful hints for a quiet, restful night's sleep.

♦ Sleep in a cool, well-ventilated room. Research has shown that sleep is less disturbed at cooler temperatures. We therefore suggest that you lower your bedroom temperature at night, the ideal being between 64 to 66° F (18 to 20° C).

♦ Darken your room by drawing the blinds or drapes. If necessary, wear comfortable eye shades. Your eyes are able to sense light even with the lids closed. Light stimuli, therefore, may prevent you from falling asleep or may interrupt deep, restful sleep.

♦ Try and eliminate any external noise or intrusive sounds preventing you from falling asleep. Comfortable, soft earplugs may be of benefit if you are forced to sleep in noisy surroundings. Listen to soft relaxing music or play tapes of soothing natural sounds if you have trouble falling asleep.

♦ Eat meals at the same time every day, including your days off. This helps maintain your natural, biological sleep/wake rhythm.

♦ Try and avoid heavy meals too soon before going to bed. The extra load placed on your digestive system will prevent you from getting a good night's rest. A glass of warm milk at bedtime can promote a restful night's sleep; it is rich in tryptophan, a naturally occurring amino acid which acts as a mild sedative. Conversely, don't go to bed hungry; you will only awaken in a couple of hours wanting to raid the refrigerator.

♦ Avoid coffee and other caffeine-containing substances before going to sleep. Tea, most colas and other soft drinks (and some medications) contain caffeine. These are stimulants which may very well interfere with your normal sleep.

♦ High-protein foods and leafy green vegetables such as broccoli and cabbage may produce excess gas, obviously interfering with sleep. Try and eat these foods in moderation, avoiding those substances in your diet which you know disturbs your sleep.

♦ Try and exercise daily or every other day. Schedule exercise periods for the late afternoon or early evening.

Strenuous exercise immediately before sleep stimulates both the nervous and cardiovascular systems, promoting wakefulness. If possible, exercise at the same time each day. This will help you to maintain a regular sleep/wake rhythm.

♦ Sleep on a firm mattress with a low pillow to keep your neck straight, reducing obstruction in your airway. Using extra pillows tends to flex the neck, effectively narrowing your upper air passages.

♦ If you suffer from any nasal congestion at night, try elevating the head of your bed by placing several books or wooden blocks under the mattress.

♦ A number of anti-snoring pillows are commercially available and are certainly worth trying. They are designed to cradle your head on its side, therefore preventing you from sleeping on your back.

A more sophisticated version of these anti-snoring pillows has recently appeared on the market in the USA. Known as PillowPositive, this pillow has a number of innovative features including a concave cradle design for maximum airway capacity in supine sleeping positions, sloped side-panel surface for alignment of head, neck and shoulders in side-sleeping positions together with ear wells to relieve ear pressure during sleeping.

Studies conducted at Stanford University show a reduction in snoring and improvement in sleep-disordered breathing using this device compared with conventional pillows.

♦ Sew a pocket between the shoulders of a pajama top or T-shirt and insert a golf or tennis ball. This is the snore-ball method, and though no clinical tests have been made of this technique, word of mouth confirms its success for some snorers.

## Smoking

In my specialty of otolaryngology, we see the harmful effects of smoking on the lining of the upper respiratory system. Smoking contributes to snoring in a number of ways:

♦ Increased production of mucus in your nose and throat.

♦ Irritation and swelling in the mucous membranes of your throat and upper air passages.

♦ Lung irritation with increased bronchial secretions.

♦ Reduced oxygen uptake by the lungs.

I strongly recommend that a snorer who smokes reduce or totally eliminate this habit as part of any self-help program to curb snoring.

## Alcohol

All snorees can describe in colorful terms the exaggerated snoring after their partner has been drinking. Alcohol is a potent central nervous system depressant which deepens sleep, increases muscle relaxation and aggravates snoring.

♦ In a scientific study, a series of middle-aged men who seldom snored, began to do so after drinking substantial amounts of alcohol.

♦ Alcohol has produced apneas in heavy snorers who previously did not have this problem.

♦ A group of patients with mild sleep apnea showed an increase in both the frequency and severity of their apneas (as recorded in a sleep center) after consuming measured amounts of alcohol.

♦ Alcohol reduces muscle activity in the upper respiratory tract, making those muscles which stabilize the pharynx more prone to vibration and collapse.

♦ Alcohol depresses the arousal response in the breathing center of the brain stem, making it less sensitive to the reduced oxygen and increased carbon dioxide which accompany sleep apnea.

Based on our knowledge derived from these studies, we can offer the following advice to the snorer and snoree:

- Avoid the habit of an alcoholic nightcap before bed.
- Mild snorers should drink only in moderation.
- Heavy snorers and those with sleep apnea should abstain from or drastically reduce their alcohol consumption.

### Over-the-Counter Medications

Billions of dollars are spent every year buying over-the-counter medications to relieve of nasal congestion. Unfortunately, many of these drugs contain antihistamines, which are central nervous system depressants, whose effects on the brain are similar to alcohol.

In addition to nasal drops and sprays, oral decongestants are widely-used medications. Because decongestants (which act by shrinking nasal blood vessels) may have stimulant side-effects, they are often combined with antihistamines. These *compound decongestants*, as they are called, are among the most frequently purchased over-the-counter medications. Most antihistamines produce some drowsiness, varying widely among individuals. Some of the newer antihistamine/decongestants with fewer sedative side-effects are available only by prescription. All of these medications can affect respiration and therefore should be used with caution if you have a sleep-related breathing disorder.

As part of your treatment program, be sure to tell your physician if you are using any nasal sprays, aspirin or other over-the-counter medications. Some of these may be exacerbating your snoring and might possibly be replaced by treatments with fewer side-effects.

### Weight Loss

We discussed the relationship between weight gain, snoring and sleep apnea in an earlier chapter. Though all of the exact mechanisms have not been yet determined, obesity is known to increase snoring and apnea for the following reasons:

♦ The increased tissue bulk in the neck and throat of obese people, together with poor muscle tone, obstructs part of your upper air passages.

♦ A large abdomen pressing on your diaphragm when lying supine increases the likelihood of sleep apnea by further decreasing the size of your lungs and the amount of air obtained with each breath.

While we cannot state the exact amount of weight loss required, we do know that stringent weight reduction can diminish and sometimes completely eliminate both snoring and sleep apnea.

♦ Sleep studies in obese patients have demonstrated that weight loss of at least 15 to 25 percent of body weight can eliminate apnea or significantly reduce the episodes.

♦ A study in markedly obese men who were double their ideal body weight showed a decrease in the average number of apneas from 70 per hour to less than 10 per hour after losing 30 to 60 percent of their original weight.

If you are overweight, it's clear that a weight-control program is a *very* important step in your efforts to stop snoring. Nutrition counselors have developed some basic rules to follow:

♦ Know your facts as you count your calories. Become familiar with the percentages of fats, carbohydrates and proteins in your regular diet. Learn about caloric values and read labels carefully. Attend weight-control classes at community hospitals. Ask your doctor for brochures, booklets or reference books on nutrition, diet and caloric values of foods.

♦ Develop calorie-consciousness. Measure portions accurately and truthfully, replacing those high-calorie foods currently in your diet with foods of lower caloric value.

♦ Limit your fat calories to less than 30 percent of your total caloric intake each day.

♦ Try to avoid heavy meals at night. If possible, eat your main meal during the day. Never eat to the point of feeling bloated and uncomfortable.

♦ Avoid food fads. Watch out for diet pills and other gimmicks often advertised with a guarantee of easy, quick weight-loss.

♦ Incorporate diet *and* exercise into your lifestyle. Regular exercise is an essential part of any weight-control program. Dieting alone tends to focus on reducing the lean muscle mass rather than the fat content of your body.

♦ Make judicious use of support groups and weight-loss programs supervised by qualified nutritionists, with the understanding that dieting is essentially a new way of life for adopting healthier eating habits.

Admittedly, starting a diet and staying with it is not easy. For heavy snorers and those with apnea, this is particularly difficult, because sleep apnea sufferers experience repeated periods of oxygen starvation. Because of their constant tiredness, these snorers have low energy levels. This limits their ability to maintain a regular exercise schedule, often producing the "vicious cycle" shown on the opposite page.

If you are caught in this cycle and are becoming discouraged in your efforts to diet and exercise, don't lose hope. Later in this chapter I will discuss some treatment options which can help you break this pattern.

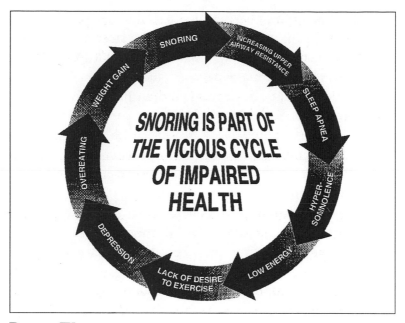

SNORING IS PART OF *THE VICIOUS CYCLE* OF IMPAIRED HEALTH

SNORING · INCREASING UPPER AIRWAY RESISTANCE · SLEEP APNEA · HYPER-SOMNOLENCE · LOW ENERGY · LACK OF DESIRE TO EXERCISE · DEPRESSION · OVEREATING · WEIGHT GAIN

## Drug Therapy

The medical profession is currently studying the use of drug therapy to treat snoring and sleep apnea, but have not found uniform success with any one drug. Some medications with theoretical benefits have turned out to be disappointing in practice. Others have unpleasant or even dangerous side-effects. But the field of drug therapy holds promise and a number of medications have shown some benefits.

Medications currently prescribed include drugs that do the following:

- Open the nasal air passages.
- Stimulate respiration.
- Promote wakefulness.
- Inhibit the rapid eye movement (REM) sleep stage.

Let's consider each group of medications—when they're indicated, their benefits and their side effects.

## Drugs That Open the Nasal Air Passages

As we have seen, nasal congestion can cause or aggravate snoring. Over-the-counter nasal decongestant drops and sprays may clear your nasal passages allowing you to breathe easier for a while, but they may, unfortunately, have some rebound effects. The chemicals in nose drops relieve congestion by constricting nasal blood vessels and shrinking your swollen mucous membranes. Shortly after application, however, the blood vessels expand again; mucous membranes begin to swell. With repeated use, these membranes lose their ability to react, remaining in a permanently swollen, congested state. We therefore recommend that decongestant drops or sprays be used for no more than two or three consecutive days.

Here are my impressions of some other available products to relieve congestion.

**Saline sprays** to moisten mucous membranes are widely available, containing nothing more than salt water. They have no ill-effects on your nasal mucous membranes. A word of caution here: Don't make your own spray. It is tempting to add a few teaspoons of salt to a bottle of water and make up your own formula, but I recommend against it. Purchase the commercial saline nasal sprays because they contain the same proportion of salt to water as your body's blood plasma. If you should put too much salt in your homemade remedy, it might burn your nose or interfere with the desired moisturizing effect.

**A new homeopathic nose drop** consisting of natural herbal ingredients was developed in China and is now available in the U.S. A clinical trial of this product, essentially a mild decongestant, conducted at Stanford University, showed a 65% reduction in the frequency and volume of snoring subjects. Marketed as *Y-Snore*, this nasal homeopathic medication can be used in drop or spray form. It appears to be completely safe and is available over-the-counter.

**Synthetic cortisone nasal sprays** have proven extremely valuable for treating seasonal hay fever as well as perennial nasal allergies, often reducing the snoring which accompanies the increased congestion. In my opinion, these medications are simple and safe to use. Clinical studies show few of the side-effects associated with systemic cortisone medications. These nasal steroid sprays, however, must be prescribed by a physician.

## Drugs That Stimulate Respiration

Many medications used to treat lung conditions, such as asthma, have also been suggested for snoring and sleep apnea.

**Progesterone.** During pregnancy and certain phases of the menstrual cycle, a woman's rate and depth of breathing increases. Researchers have been able to produce a similar effect in men by giving them progesterone (a female sex hormone). This drug, therefore, has been prescribed for certain types of sleep apnea. It works, in theory, by stimulating the breathing center in the brain and by redistributing body fat.

*Indications:* Progesterone has been most successful in treating overweight, severe snorers with predominately central apnea.

*Side effects:* These include hair loss, impotence and reduced sex drive. These effects usually reverse when the drug is discontinued or if male hormones are administered. Progesterone may produce uterine bleeding in postmenopausal females or aggravate growths of the prostate gland in elderly males. This drug should not be used in patients with a history of liver disease or blood-clotting disorders.

**Acetazolamide.** This drug acts on the kidneys, stimulating respiration by increasing blood-acidity. This chemical reaction is known as *metabolic acidosis.*

*Indications:* This drug has been used in cases of central

apnea with occasional beneficial effects. However, there are no reports of its success for obstructive sleep apnea.

*Side effects:* Numbness, tingling in the hands and feet, drowsiness and confusion. This drug should not be used in any patient with liver or kidney disease.

**Theophylline.** Frequently prescribed for asthma, this drug stimulates breathing by its effects on the respiratory center in the brain stem.

*Indications:* Theophylline has not shown much promise in treating sleep apnea, but may be of some benefit in central apnea.

*Side effects:* Nausea, mental irritability and cardiac arrhythmias.

## Drugs That Promote Wakefulness

**Amphetamines.** Although they have no direct effect on sleep apnea, stimulants can provide symptomatic relief from excess daytime sleepiness (EDS). They should be prescribed for short periods only, when other medical therapies are unsuccessful or for patients who refuse any type of mechanical or surgical treatment. Side-effects include anxiety, agitation, insomnia and weight-loss. Of course, amphetamines are addictive and are therefore prescribed very judiciously.

## Drugs That Inhibit the REM Sleep Stage

Because most severe snoring and sleep apnea occur during REM sleep, drugs which shorten this phase of your sleep cycle can theoretically diminish the incidence of apnea.

**Protriptyline.** The most commonly prescribed drug for sleep apnea associated with daytime sleepiness, this medication inhibits REM sleep.

*Indications:* Protriptyline has been used by patients with sleep apnea complicated by excessive daytime sleepiness.

*Side effects:* Dry mouth, urinary retention and cardiac arrhythmias. This drug can increase muscle movement (especially leg movement) during sleep. It should not be used by patients over 60 years of age, those who are overweight or those with any psychological or emotional disorders.

# A Homeopathic Medication for Snoring

A new homeopathic remedy for snoring has recently been introduced in the United States. Developed by a Portland naturopathic physician, Kenneth H. Rifkin, N.D., and marketed as *Snore Stop*, this product appears to be a safe and effective treatment for non-apneic snoring.

Available over-the-counter, *Snore Stop* contains several homeopathic pharmaceutical ingredients, designed to improve upper airway muscle tone, regulate nasal secretions as well as decreasing nasal allergic reactions.

Each tablet contains the following homeopathic ingredients: Nux vomica, Ma Huang (Teamsters tea), Histaminum hydrochloride, Teucrium marum, Hydrastis Canadensis, Atropa belladonna, Kali bichromicum.

In a double-blind clinical study, 100 snoring adults in Portland, Oregon were screened by this author. Suitable candidates were randomly given either the active ingredient or a placebo medication. There were no side-effects to either product.

Each study subject was given a snoring diary, completed by their sleepmate over 10 nights, documenting changes in the frequency and volume of their snoring. Statistical analysis indicated that the majority of subjects taking the active ingredient experienced a significant reduction in the frequency and volume of their snoring, according to their bedroom partners, compared to the placebo group.

Homeopathy is a healing art, more than 200 years old. This discipline offers a therapeutic alternative to conventional medicine, helping natural body mechanisms correct underlying dysfunctions by using highly diluted microscopic doses of natural substances.

## An External Nasal Dilator

Worn over your nose like an adhesive plaster, this mechanical device gently pulls the nasal walls outward, improving airflow by expanding your nasal passages.

One study testing the efficacy of this nasal dilator, at the University of Arkansas for Medical Sciences, showed increased nasal airflow. Another study in heavy snorers demonstrated reduced snoring volumes in more than 70 percent of subjects.

Approved by the FDA, the external nasal dilator is now available over-the-counter as a safe treatment for snoring, before seeking medical advice. If, however, you have any symptoms of sleep apnea, you should consult a physician, have an examination of your upper airway and, if indicated, an overnight sleep study.

## Mouth Appliances to Expand the Upper Airway

What if lifestyle modifications or medications as measures against snoring and apnea are not suitable or do not work for you? A number of oral (mouth) appliances, now available, might prove beneficial.

Two basic types of oral appliances are currently available. The first is called a *tongue retaining device*; the second is known as a *mandibular (jaw) repositioning appliance*.

The first tongue retaining device for sleep-induced upper airway obstruction was introduced in 1980 by Rosalind Cartwright, Ph.D., and Charles Samelson, M.D., of Chicago, Illinois. Made of a soft plastic material attaching to the tongue by suction, this device pulls the tongue forward, while simultaneously widening the pharyngeal airway. Severe snorers and sleep apnea sufferers can learn to sleep with this appliance in position for three or four hours each night. However, discomfort or eventual loss of suction sometimes prevents the wearer from using it for longer periods.

Appliances in this category are sometimes recommended for severe snorers and for those with sleep apnea who cannot tolerate other treatments and refuse to have corrective surgery. The results of a clinical trial, published in 1982, showed a substantial reduction in both snoring and sleep apnea. The majority of patients in this trial also reported relief from their daytime sleepiness.

The second type of oral appliance is known as a *mandibular repositioning device*. These appliances fit firmly over your teeth and expand the pharyngeal airway by advancing your jaw. Despite variations in design, their basic function is to hold the lower jaw forward, and by doing so, enlarge your airway.

Mandibular repositioning devices are made from a variety of dental materials, held in place by wire loops fitting over your teeth or by frictional fit. To demonstrate the benefits of such treatment, one type of heat-molded oral appliance, introduced by Dr. Veres, a South African dental surgeon, in a recent clinical trial, reduced snoring in 77 percent of subjects.

Since mandibular repositioning appliances move your lower jaw forward, holding it there for many hours of sleep, they should be used with caution in patients having a history of temporomandibular joint problems. The effects on the jaw joint should be continuously monitored in all patients using this appliance.

One of the earliest of these devices was developed at the University of New Mexico by Wolfgang W. Schmidt-Nowara, M.D., and Thomas Meade, D.D.S. Their appliance can be fitted by any trained dentist; many wearers say that they can use it comfortably throughout the night. In a clinical trial with patients having mild to moderate sleep apnea, 80 percent were successful in curbing their apnea and reducing daytime sleepiness.

But it should be understood that this device is only one of some 30 mandibular repositioning appliances currently on the market, varying in design, material and adjustability. Different designs of appliances vary in both effectiveness and trauma to the temporomandibular joint.

Tongue retaining devices and mandibular repositioning appliances can be effective in different people. A trial period is therefore often necessary to determine which oral appliance is the most effective for an individual patient. This obviously requires the services of a dentist familiar with many types of oral appliances.

If you are considering mouth appliance therapy for snoring or sleep apnea, here are my recommendations:

**Have a complete upper airway examination followed by an overnight sleep study, if appropriate, to determine whether you suffer from sleep apnea.** Your physician should determine whether you have a clear nasal airway. Medical treatment or sometimes surgery may be required to clear your nasal passages before using any oral appliance.

**Consult with a dentist having expertise in the field of snoring and sleep apnea.** Ideally, you should seek dental therapy from a dentist with special training in sleep disorders, familiar with the techniques of fitting several types of oral appliances; and preferably has a close working relationship with a nearby sleep disorders center. Do not hesitate to ask your dentist about his/her special training and education in sleep-breathing disorders through courses or seminars.

**Obtain a proper fit.** Mouth appliances are usually fitted by dentists with special training in these fitting techniques. Your regular dentist, therefore, may not be familiar with them. However, the medical director of your local sleep disorders center should know about these prostheses and recommend a suitable dental practitioner for you. Your local dental society should be able to provide you with names of dentists interested in sleep disorders; the appendix contains the address and telephone number of the Sleep Disorders Dental Society, who can provide a similar service.

**Ask about the cost**. Some appliances are relatively simple, requiring no more than one or two visits to a dentist for fitting. Others, requiring multiple visits, can prove to be quite expensive.

**Keep an open mind**. Understand that there will be some initial discomfort while wearing an oral appliance and that a learning period is necessary before you can use it comfortably.

Prosthetic oral appliances are valuable indicators when jaw surgery is being considered. If they are of benefit, then surgery may be helpful. These devices are also useful for patients whose general health makes surgery inadvisable or for those who have had upper airway surgery, with limited success. Even if an oral appliance is not completely successful in relieving all your snoring or apnea, it may be used on an occasional basis. A patient using nasal continuous positive airway pressure (more about this later in the chapter) for example, may temporarily use an oral appliance while traveling or camping, when a CPAP unit could not be used.

Oral appliance therapy should be undertaken by a dentist who is willing to become part of a treatment team, which includes a physician trained in sleep disorders. I strongly recommend that you avoid any device that is available over-the-counter, because snoring, as we know by now, can be the sign of a more serious medical disorder.

Furthermore, such an appliance, sold and utilized without medical supervision, can cause serious problems to your jaw joint.

These appliances were never intended to cure every case of sleep apnea. If, after a trial period, the appliance still makes you gag and disturbs your sleep, or if it does not appear to help either your snoring and apnea symptoms, feel free to say so and discuss other options of treatment with your doctors.

## Nasal Continuous Positive Airway Pressure

In 1981, Dr. Colin Sullivan, a lung specialist at the University of Sydney, Australia, introduced a new method for treating sleep apnea, eliminating upper airway collapse by pumping a constant stream of air into the nose and throat during sleep.

Referred to as *nasal continuous positive airway pressure* (nasal CPAP; pronounced "see-pap"), this device pumps air under sufficient pressure to expand the collapsed airway. This technique, also called *pneumatic splinting of the pharynx*, was introduced into the United States in 1984.

Recommended for patients diagnosed with obstructive sleep apnea by an overnight sleep study, nasal continuous positive airway pressure (CPAP) is now the treatment of choice at sleep disorders centers. Because of its success in eradicating the obstructed breathing of sleep apnea, CPAP is now prescribed with increasing enthusiasm by sleep disorders specialists throughout this country, and in fact, the world. We estimate that more than 200,000 people throughout the United States regularly use CPAP while sleeping.

A nasal CPAP unit resembles a small computer terminal. The whole apparatus weighs about 10 pounds, al-

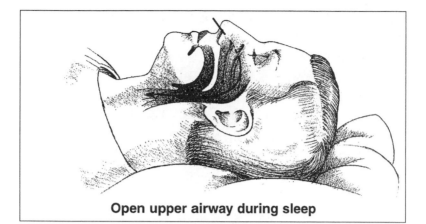

**Open upper airway during sleep**

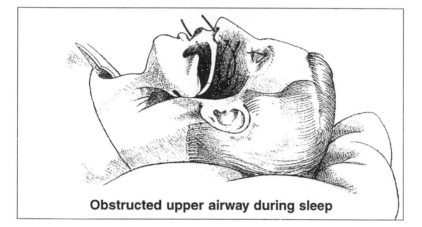

**Obstructed upper airway during sleep**

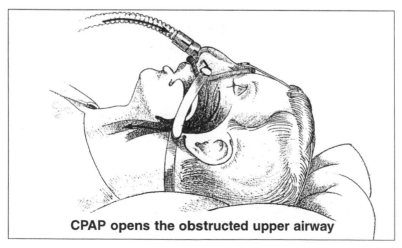

**CPAP opens the obstructed upper airway**

though lighter, more portable units are now available. This unit typically includes the following components:

+ An air pressure turbine or fan called a *blower*.

+ A soft, pliable mask fitting snugly over the nose, held onto the head with straps; or a device holding soft cushioned tubes against each nostril.

+ A valve-assembly control to adjust or maintain air pressure at the desired level.

+ A flexible tube or hose connecting the blower to the nose mask.

## How Is a CPAP Unit Fitted?

After your initial sleep test, you will have to spend another night in the sleep disorders center with all the sensors applied, as for a regular sleep study. Your technician will describe and demonstrate the CPAP equipment. A soft silicone mask is fitted comfortably over your nose, firmly enough to prevent air leaks.

Once asleep, the sleep technician slowly adjusts the valve on the blower unit, gradually increasing air pressure going into your nose. Pressure is increased until your repeated apneas are eliminated. You then spend the night sleeping with CPAP applied, while the technician periodically checks to ensure that your apneas do not recur. This process of determining your specific CPAP pressure requirement is called *CPAP titration*.

A new method of CPAP fitting or titration, known as a *split-night study*, is now being widely applied. Using this technique, CPAP is introduced on the same night as your initial sleep test. In other words, once sleep apnea is recorded (after 3 or 4 hours) CPAP is applied and the necessary adjustments made. Clinical studies confirm the accuracy of this titration method compared with the traditional two-night technique.

Once you make the decision to use CPAP, your physi-

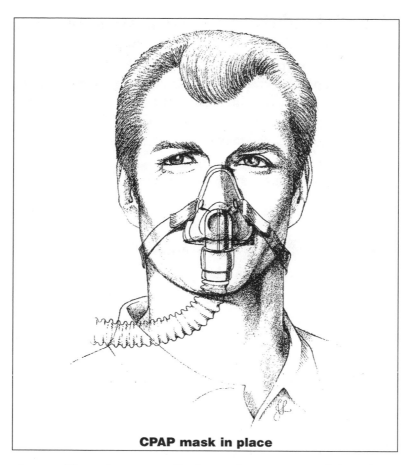

**CPAP mask in place**

cian notifies a home medical supply company, giving them details of mask size and recommended pressures. You can rent a CPAP unit and if satisfied with the results, you may buy your own machine. Rental fees are usually applied to the purchase price.

After you have been titrated for CPAP and you have brought a unit home, follow-up will usually be arranged by your sleep disorders center personnel. In most centers, a nurse coordinates appointments, answering questions about the use and maintenance of your CPAP machine.

Your partner's support is an essential component to successfully using CPAP. Understanding the benefits to your health and witnessing the obvious improvement in energy and mood, usually offsets any reluctance by your mate to accept CPAP into the bedroom.

There is now a nationwide network of support groups for sleep apnea sufferers using CPAP. Your sleep disorders staff will put you in touch with the nearest A.W.A.K.E. group (Alive, Well, And Keeping Energetic). These groups meet regularly to provide support and education for sleep apnea patients and their family members. The address and telephone number of the A.W.A.K.E. network is listed in the appendix.

## Who Can Benefit from CPAP?

CPAP is the preferred initial treatment for patients diagnosed with any significant degree of sleep apnea. It is especially useful for those with oxygen desaturation or debilitating daytime sleepiness. CPAP is also extremely helpful for obese patients with sleep apnea; for the first time in years they can achieve restful sleep. The newly-found daytime vigor gives them the motivation and energy to lose weight by diligently pursuing a supervised weight control/exercise program.

CPAP is rarely recommended for severe snorers who do not have sleep apnea, yet reject other forms of treatment. Similarly, those diagnosed with the upper airway resistance syndrome (discussed in an earlier chapter) can also benefit, but because apnea is not manifest, titration is very difficult.

Nasal CPAP has been prescribed for patients diagnosed with central sleep apnea. Surprisingly, many of these respond very well to this form of treatment. These patients are therefore now being referred to as having *central-like apnea* and are designated as *positive CPAP responders*. Finally, CPAP is occasionally used after surgery, in the immediate postoperative period, to counteract swelling in the throat.

# What are the advantages and disadvantages of CPAP?

Treatment for sleep apnea with nasal CPAP is, for the most part, safe and effective. Apnea patients report a restful night's sleep, for the first time in years, with relief of daytime sleepiness.

CPAP, however, is not a cure for sleep apnea; it only works if you use it every night. Poor sleep quality and daytime sleepiness all rapidly recur with discontinued use.

Useful and effective as it is, not every sleep apnea patient can or wants to use CPAP for the rest of their days. There are, unfortunately, some negative aspects to CPAP treatment. Here are some of these disadvantages:

- Quite a few patients report feelings of claustrophobia when first using CPAP. Because of this problem, some simply cannot tolerate its long-term use.

- The headgear used to secure the CPAP mask may be uncomfortable or produce excess sweating, especially during warm summer nights.

- Some patients experience a dry mouth, eye irritation or ear infections resulting from air being blown into their nose throughout the night.

- The noise of a CPAP unit may disturb a light-sleeping partner, although the latest models function very quietly.

- People with severe nasal obstructions, due to nasal polyps or a deviated septum, for example, may have difficulty in adapting to CPAP.

- Partners of some patients on CPAP, especially those in new relationships, may have an initial loss of romantic feelings. These concerns are often overcome with regained energy and elimination of snoring.

- A CPAP unit is an additional piece of baggage when you travel. It may also pose problems when used on airplanes or in foreign countries.

♦ Some medical conditions, for example over-inflated, weak lungs or chronic ear infections may limit CPAP usage.

For one or several of these reasons, some patients will refuse to accept CPAP as long-term treatment for their sleep apnea. In fact, clinical studies on long-term CPAP compliance show that approximately 30 percent of patients are unable or unwilling to regularly use their CPAP units at night.

Regular follow-up by your sleep disorders center, minor adjustments to your mask and pressure unit, attendance at support group meetings and an understanding that CPAP is a lifesaver should all serve to improve your long-term compliance.

## Care and Feeding of Your CPAP Machine

The treatment of sleep apnea with nasal CPAP is essentially safe and simple, once you understand its working principles. However, some ongoing maintenance is required. For a more detailed discussion of CPAP maintenance and troubleshooting, I recommend an excellent book, *Phantom of the Night* by T. Scott Johnson, M.D. and Jerry Halberstadt (New Technology Publishing, Cambridge, Massachusetts 1995).

The following section touches briefly on some commonly raised issues of nasal CPAP use:

### Setting up Your CPAP Unit

Your CPAP plugs directly into the wall electric outlet. A surge protector will protect against any alteration in current. Keep your CPAP close to the bed, either on the floor or on a low table, ensuring adequate slack in both the power line and air hose.

Masks should be cleaned after use with mild detergents,

**Nasal CPAP in use during sleep**

rinsed and then reattached to the air hose. By switching on the blower, the mask will dry between uses.

We advise that manufacturer's maintenance manuals and cleaning instructions be carefully followed. Slight technical differences may exist between different makes and models.

### Power Failure

Although not absolutely necessary, you can keep a stand-by battery ready in the event of a power failure.

### Masks

CPAP masks are now available in various styles. These include nasal masks, nasal cushions and full-face masks. Preference for any particular type is largely a matter of trial and error. There are wide variations in styles and models. Therefore, by trying a variety of masks attached to different harnesses and headgear, you can ultimately achieve a comfortable fit. Irrespective of the make or model, a mask should fit snugly, yet without any obvious air leak.

### Noise

There is no such thing as a completely silent CPAP unit. Remember that the early models were based on vacuum cleaner motors, set in reverse. We have come a long way since then. The newer models now run very quietly, but can still be heard, especially by a partner who is a light sleeper. Without question, the mild noise generated by your CPAP is less disturbing than the familiar sound of loud snoring and choking associated with sleep apnea.

Maintaining your CPAP machine in good mechanical condition with regular servicing and cleaning reduces noise levels to their minimum.

### Changing The CPAP Pressure

As you know, you have undergone CPAP titration to determine the amount of positive pressure required to overcome your apnea. These pressure settings, measured in centimeters of water, vary from a low of 5 centimeters to higher pressures of 15 or 16 centimeters of water.

Some situations, however, can alter your CPAP pressure requirements. Weight gain, for example, may require higher pressures. Conversely, weight loss may allow you to breathe comfortably at lower pressures. Any central nervous system depressants, antihistamines or tranquilizers may produce added relaxation, hence higher pressure requirements. Alcohol, as stated earlier, has the same effect.

Patients on CPAP are discouraged from changing the pressure settings themselves. After the initial calibration, a technician is required to make appropriate adjustments if you are uncomfortable with your current pressure level.

### Humidity

Many patients using CPAP complain about dry eyes or mouth from the constant air flow. A number of simple remedies may help. Saline nasal sprays are useful and are purchased at low prices over-the-counter. I encourage using a separate humidifier in your bedroom, although some CPAP units have their own built-in humidifiers.

### Traveling

Some newer CPAP models are now of sufficiently small size and weight to be carried around comfortably while traveling. These can usually be stored safely within the cabin of an airplane. You may be asked to check you CPAP at airport security. Explain that it's a medical device for a breathing disorder. Should security personnel insist on sending your CPAP through an x-ray scanner, no mechanical harm will be done. When traveling to foreign countries, I recommend having a letter from your doctor explaining the need of this machine for medical purposes. When traveling by train, your CPAP can be plugged into the electrical outlets in most railroad sleeping cars.

Although most sleep apnea patients can go without CPAP for a number of hours, you may wish to use it on a long and tiring airplane flight. If so, I suggest that you make prior arrangements with the airline, discussing the specific power supply of your machine.

### Camping

You can power your CPAP on camping trips with a special deep-cycle battery. By doing so, you can enjoy the outdoors *and* get a decent night's rest.

### Medical Insurance

Sleep studies, CPAP titration and rental or purchase of a CPAP unit are all usually covered by the majority of medical insurance plans. An appropriate letter from your sleep disorders physician will support your claim. ICD-9 and CPT codes relevant to sleep-related breathing disorders and their treatment are listed in the appendix to assist you with your medical insurance claims.

## Better CPAP Tolerance Through Hypnosis

Compliance is perhaps the biggest hurdle to overcome in using nasal CPAP. One recent technique, according to Martin S. Pollens, a clinical hypnotist, is that of hypnosis to improve user compliance.

Hypnosis, a state of altered consciousness, is now being applied to overcome the fear and anxiety often accompanying CPAP, especially for new users.

- ♦ **Amnesia:** Helping a patient forget an unpleasnat memory or experience.

- ♦ **Distraction:** Leading attention away from negative, annoying aspects of an experience towards more positive, pleasing ones.

- ♦ **Suggestion:** A technique for introducing a change of attitude or reaction to any given experience.

- ♦ **Time Distortion:** Helping patients perceive unpleasant experiences as shorter; good experiences as longer.

- ♦ **Reframing:** Helping transform a negative experience into a more positive one by a change in attitude or by better understanding.

# Advances in CPAP Technology

In the search towards improved compliance, nasal CPAP technology has made great strides since its introduction here a mere decade ago.

One recent refinement of CPAP is a variable pressure pump called *bi-level CPAP*. Unlike CPAP, which exerts a constant air pressure through the nose during inhalation and exhalation, this biphasic device is better tolerated, especially by obese patients or those with any muscle weakness.

Another improvement in CPAP technology is the recent addition of a *ramp* function, also known as *adjustable pressure delay*. This allows the prescribed CPAP pressure to be gradually achieved, usually over 30 or 40 minutes. The gradual pressure build-up is more comfortable; the patient is often asleep by the time full pressure is developed.

A recent development and one holding a great deal of promise for the future, incorporates an interactive system which senses and then provides, on demand, the exact amount of pressure required to open the collapsed airway. As we have mentioned, these pressure requirements will vary according to body positions or depth of sleep.

A sleep apnea sufferer himself, Joseph Goldstein invented CPAP/PRO®, a method of holding the nasal puffs in alignment by a pliable dental appliance, fixed to the upper teeth. This method eliminates the need for headstraps to keep the nasal cushions in place.

Dr. William P. Hart, a Stanford Sleep Disorders Clinic researcher and lung specialist, recently introduced a refinement called an Oral Pressure Appliance (OPAP®). Applied to the mouth like a specialized mouth-guard, OPAP positions the lower jaw forward, effectively combining two therapies into one device.

This method of oral rather than nasal air delivery eliminates the need for head gear, straps, and nasal masks or cushions. Additionally, lower CPAP pressure is needed to splint the pharynx since this method bypasses the nasal and sinus passages as well as stabilizing the jaw during sleep.

The above refinements, incorporated into the new generation of CPAP units can now make this form of treatment for sleep apnea more tolerable to a greater number of patients.

Admittedly, despite these technological advances, CPAP requires some getting used to. But patients who persevere usually obtain immediate improvement in their symptoms.

For many, however, such perseverance is not always practical or possible. CPAP, as we have mentioned, is rarely the treatment of choice for a heavy snorer without symptoms of sleep apnea.

Surgical methods, therefore, are the next treatment options to consider in order to silence snorers and bring some rest to their disturbed (and disturbing) nights.

## Surgery For Snoring and Sleep Apnea

Although physicians recognized many years ago that the vibrating uvula and soft palate were the noisy culprits of snoring, early attempts to excise these offending organs or somehow stiffen them, proved ineffective. In fact, the uvula has been regarded as something of a redundant vestigial organ, without any special function.

Surgeons in Italy, more than 300 years ago, removed uvulas for symptoms as divergent as bed-wetting and insomnia, despite any real scientific basis for their operations. George Bernard Shaw, a card-carrying cynic, in *The Doctor's Dilemma*, describes a Dr. Walpole, who blithely snipped off patients' uvulas for 50 guineas, with no apparent benefit to their owners.

Dr. Marcus H. Boulware, our pioneer snoring researcher, described his own desperate efforts to find a snoring cure—even convincing a surgeon to remove his uvula. In Dr. Boulware's book, *Snoring: New Answers to an Old Problem*, the author states that surgical removal of the uvula has been discontinued, because of poor results, for more than 100 years.

In 1942, Dr. Jerome Strauss of Chicago treated seven unrepentant snorers, injecting their uvulas with sylnasol, a chemical which stimulates scarring. He was successful in only one case; the other six refused further treatment. This setback obviously defused further efforts to scar and stiffen the uvulas of uncontrolled snorers on any universal scale.

Ten years later, a Japanese physician, Dr. Kubomura of Taihoko Imperial University Hospital, attempted to cure two patients by injecting paraffin into their soft palates. Although his efforts met with some success, this procedure was not made available to the public for lack of further clinical trials.

A modern version of this technique, called Injection Snoreplasty, developed by researchers at Walter Reed Medical Center, is currently under trial. The early reports appear to be very promising.

Modern surgical treatment to relieve snoring was started in Japan in 1952 by Dr. Takenosuke Ikematsu, who rightfully deserves the title "Father of Snoring". He cured a young bride whose marriage was threatened by her violent snoring, by removing excess tissue from her throat.

Inspired by his initial success, Dr. Ikematsu treated more patients whose snoring had disrupted their relationships. In 1964 he reported the results of his surgical treatment for 152 habitual snorers. During the next four years, this intrepid surgeon studied upper airway anatomy in 300 habitual snorers, attempting to correlate sound with structure. Continuing to perform these surgeries, he reported his success rate of over 80 percent in the medical literature. Dr. Ikematsu called these surgeries *palatectomy* and *partial uvulectomy*, effectively removing some soft palate tissue together with part of the uvula, thus enlarging the throat.

The groundwork by this insightful surgeon set the stage for a new surgical procedure, introduced into the United States in 1980 by Shiro Fujita, M.D., at the Henry Ford Hospital in Detroit, Michigan. His operation, called *uvulopalatopharyngoplasty*—which, according to some surgeons, is easier to perform than to pronounce—enlarges a patient's pharynx by removing the uvula, tonsils and part of the soft palate. Abbreviated as *UPPP* or *UP3*, Dr. Fujita's surgery is today the most commonly performed for severe snoring, associated with obstructive sleep apnea.

Similar surgical techniques, also based on Dr. Ikematsu's original work, were being applied at the same time by F. Blair Simmons, M.D., at Stanford University School of Medicine. He and Dr. Fujita taught UPPP techniques to surgeons throughout the country, publishing papers on this procedure and its results. Their efforts have led to courses and seminars—often presented by sleep disorders centers—where surgeons are taught these surgical techniques while learning about the clinical aspects of sleep apnea and overnight sleep testing.

Another major advance in the relentless search for a snoring cure was made as recently as 1990 when Dr. Yves-Victor Kamami, a French surgeon, published a paper describing an office-based laser surgery for snoring.

Known as *laser-assisted uvulopalatoplasty* (LAUP), this procedure, performed under local anesthetic, now represents a quick, safe and effective snoring cure. Two years later, Swedish surgeons reported successful results with a similar laser surgery. By the following year, LAUP was widely practiced by ear, nose and throat specialists in cities across the United States.

A single operation certainly cannot do the job for all snorers or those with sleep apnea, as obstructions may occur in several areas of the upper airway, some requiring more than one surgery. When a patient needs multiple surgeries—called *revision of the upper airway*—these may be performed in stages or in one session, depending on the scope of these procedures and the philosophy of the individual surgeon.

Irrespective of the specific details, the goal of any surgery on the upper airway is the complete elimination of snoring and, if present, all symptoms of sleep apnea—without interfering with the patient's essential functions of speech, breathing and swallowing.

It is not difficult to judge the results of surgery for snoring. Simply put, snoring is in the ear of the beholder. Your bedroom companion, therefore, will surely let you know whether your snoring has been silenced, reduced or remains unchanged by treatment.

Because some people are lighter sleepers than others, the basic yardstick for measuring the success of surgery is whether your partner can get a decent night's sleep, no longer troubled by your snoring. In other words, a good result is regarded as complete cessation of snoring or a reduction to acceptable levels which no longer disturb your bed-partner.

Measuring outcomes and success rates for the surgical treatment of sleep apnea, on the other hand, is more complex. Apart from the effect on snoring, improvement in sleep-quality and reduction in daytime sleepiness is obviously an important subjective measure of success. This, however, can be misleading. Some patients feel much better after their surgery for sleep apnea, yet postoperative sleep studies show little improvement.

Objective studies, therefore, are necessary if we are to achieve any scientific measure of success. Ideally, every patient who undergoes upper airway surgery for sleep apnea should have an overnight sleep study before *and* after surgery.

The postoperative sleep study is usually done some three or four months after surgery, allowing time for complete healing. Your physician can also supervise weight control during this postoperative period.

Surgeons treating sleep apnea patients sometimes disagree on the exact definition of surgical success. One index sometimes used is complete resolution of symptoms and a *normal* postoperative sleep study. By normal, we mean that the respiratory disturbance index (RDI) and oxygen desaturation are returned to within normal levels.

Another way of defining a successful surgical outcome is the relief of daytime symptoms and a postoperative sleep study showing reduction of the respiratory disturbance index to less than 50 percent of the preoperative value.

Postoperative sleep studies after surgery for sleep apnea, therefore, are always recommended, yet some insurance companies are reluctant to cover the costs of these tests. As a result, surgeons and sleep disorders specialists are seeking a simpler, less expensive, yet accurate way of assessing surgical results.

Irrespective of the procedure selected, good results depend upon the surgeon's ability to diagnose and isolate the exact area of obstruction in the upper airway. Careful evaluation to identify the regions of narrowing and collapse, therefore, increases the likelihood of a successful outcome. This approach is called *site-specific surgery.*

The decision to have surgery is obviously a major one and should be considered only after you have done the following:

♦ Undergone a thorough medical evaluation, including an examination of your upper respiratory tract by an otolaryngologist (ear, nose and throat specialist).

♦ Had an overnight sleep study, if this is indicated.

♦ Received a detailed explanation from your physician regarding all of the treatment options available to you.

♦ Tried lifestyle changes (including weight loss) and discussed appropriate noninvasive conservative approaches (medications, an oral appliance or nasal CPAP) with your physician.

If snoring continues to disrupt your life despite these measures or if your health is still affected by daytime sleepiness or fatigue, you should talk with your physician about surgical treatment.

We will discuss surgery for snoring and sleep apnea according to the anatomical areas involved in these procedures:

♦ Surgery of the nasal cavity (the nose and nearby structures, including the sinuses).

♦ Surgery of the nasopharynx (the area behind the nose).

♦ Surgery of the oropharynx (the throat and related structures).

♦ Surgery of the hypopharynx (the area behind and below the jaw).

♦ Surgery of the trachea (the windpipe).

**How to Use This Section**
Accepting medical treatment of any kind or undergoing surgery is a highly personal decision. You should make that decision only *after* your treating physician has fully explained all aspects of the recommended therapy or procedure, including the options, risks and potential complications of such treatment. There is a wide variety in surgical techniques, types of anesthetics and postoperative care. The duration of hospital stays varies with individual patients.

This section, therefore, serves merely as a *guide* to some of the surgical operations currently recommended and performed for snoring and sleep apnea. It is written to introduce and explain some principles and terminology of surgery on the upper airway. I recommend consulting your physician, who can then refer you to authoritative texts or papers, if you wish to have more detailed information on any particular procedure.

## Surgery of the Nasal Cavity

*Surgical operation:* Nasal septoplasty

*Definition:* An operation to improve the nasal airway by realigning the partition separating the two sides of your nose.

*Indications:* This surgery is recommended if you snore severely, have not responded to conservative treatment, and it has been determined that your airway obstruction is caused by a deviated nasal septum.

*Postoperative care:* You will probably go home on the same day as the surgery. Your surgeon removes any nasal packing within a day or two. Your nose will be congested for about a week after surgery, though by this time you will have resumed most normal activities.

*Results:* Although nasal septoplasty is usually successful in clearing the nasal airway, it is not always effective in eliminating snoring. If you continue to snore following this operation, there may be some other obstructive site in your upper respiratory tract; you will most likely be advised to undergo further evaluation.

*Surgical operation:* Turbinectomy

*Definition:* An operation to reduce the size of the turbinates, structures which lie along the inner walls of the nose and are enlarged from allergies or infection.

*Indications:* This surgery is recommended if your snoring is associated with unremitting nasal obstruction from enlarged turbinates, not responding to medical treatment.

*Postoperative care:* Postoperative care for turbinectomy is similar to that of nasal septoplasty, though more frequent follow-up visits are usually required.

*Results:* The overall results of this surgery are generally very satisfactory, with improved breathing and more restful sleep once the mucous membranes in the nose have healed. Here too, however, your snoring may continue, despite the improvement in your nasal airway.

Surgical reduction of turbinates with a *laser* is now performed as a quick, safe and effective office procedure. Laser surgery of this type, discussed in more detail in the following chapter is done under local anesthetic, virtually without discomfort, bleeding or swelling.

*Surgical operation:* Nasal polypectomy

*Definition:* An operation to remove polyps from the nose and sinuses.

*Indications:* This surgery is recommended if your snoring is caused by nasal obstruction or chronic sinus infection from nasal polyps. These waterlogged swellings arise from the mucous membrane lining of the sinuses as a result of allergy or infection. Blocked sinuses are frequently treated at the same time. Viewing the inside of the nose through a rigid *endoscope* (telescope) and using specially designed surgical instruments, the surgeon removes polyps from the sinuses, establishing natural drainage and restoring sinus function. Before surgery is considered, you should have allergy tests, if appropriate, and medical treatment—which may include antibiotics, decongestants or steroid nasal sprays.

*Postoperative care:* The care required after nasal polypectomy is similar to that of the previous surgeries. Because nasal polyps may recur, however, you will probably require periodic follow-up visits, combined with some form of anti-allergic control.

*Results:* Nasal polypectomy usually produces gratifying results, allowing a return to normal breathing. If your snoring is directly due to nasal obstruction from polyps, improvement should occur once your nasal passages are clear.

*Note:* Although surgical improvement of the nasal airway alone is usually not successful for curing sleep apnea, there is frequently subjective improvement in those cases where severe nasal obstruction existed. In addition, provision of a clear nasal airway may greatly benefit the use of nasal CPAP.

### Surgery of the Nasopharynx

*Surgical operation:* Adenoidectomy

*Definition:* A surgical procedure to remove spongy lymphoid tissue from the back of the nose.

*Indications:* Adenoidectomy is recommended for children with severe snoring, nasal obstruction and constant mouth breathing due to enlarged adenoids. This surgery is considered only when medical measures have failed and other causes of nasal congestion, including allergies, have been excluded.

*Postoperative care:* Other than a mild sore throat, the recovery tends to be quick; the child usually resumes normal activities within a day or two.

*Results:* This procedure is usually successful; the child's snoring, mouth breathing, nasal obstruction and apnea customarily resolves within days of the surgery.

*Surgical operation:* Removal of nasopharyngeal masses

*Definition:* Surgical removal of polyps, cysts or swellings from the back of the nose.

*Indications:* When it has been determined that snoring occurs from obstruction in the nasopharynx.

*Postoperative care:* Varies according to the source of the swelling and scope of the surgery performed. In most cases, recovery is rapid, with minimal discomfort; normal activities are resumed within a few days.

*Results:* Snoring usually stops after the nasal airway has been cleared, if this obstruction is the predominant cause.

## Surgery of the Oropharynx

*Surgical operation:* Tonsillectomy (in children)

*Definition:* Surgical removal of the tonsils.

*Indications:* Tonsillectomy for snoring is recommended when a child's snoring is severe and is accompanied by constant mouth breathing, frequent colds and restless sleeping; all attributed to enlarged tonsils. Often combined with adenoidectomy, removal of tonsils is recommended when symptoms of severe upper respiratory obstruction persist, despite thorough medical treatment.

*Postoperative care:* The child will have a sore throat, usually lasting four to six days, responding to pain medication, tender loving care and the traditional rewards of ice cream, Jell-O, popsicles and milkshakes.

*Results:* Snoring and apnea usually disappear shortly after surgery.

*Surgical operation:* Tonsillectomy (in adults)

*Definition:* Surgical removal of tonsils

*Indications:* Tonsillectomy for adults is performed for the same reasons as in children. Other anatomical changes, however, such as an elongated uvula or a sagging palate may contribute to both snoring and obstructive sleep apnea in adults, requiring additional surgery—the most frequently performed being uvulopalatopharyngoplasty.

*Postoperative care:* Adults do not recover quite as

quickly as children. They usually experience a painful throat for seven to ten days—requiring rest, medication and supportive care.

*Results:* Tonsillectomy alone may not cure an adult's snoring; for this reason the following procedure is sometimes performed at the same time.

### A Face-Lift on the Back of Your Throat

Because the following surgery is the most frequently performed procedure for sleep apnea, we will consider it in some detail.

*Surgical operation:* Uvulopalatopharyngoplasty (UPPP or UP3)

*Definition:* An operation to enlarge the throat (the oropharyngeal airway). By removing the tonsils, if they are still present, together with the uvula and edge of the soft palate, the surgeon expands your airway. This operation has aptly been termed a "face-lift on the back of your throat".

*Indications:* If you are a severe snorer with associated sleep apnea, confirmed on an overnight sleep study, most surgeons now agree that you can benefit from UPPP, after conservative methods of treatment have failed.

Uvulopalatopharyngoplasty for snoring without sleep apnea is rarely done. It is only considered when a patient's snoring is severe enough to threaten the intimacy of a relationship, when a couple can no longer sleep in the same room and all other treatments have failed. This surgery is usually done when the exact site of upper airway obstruction has been accurately localized to the back of the throat. Such an obstruction usually includes: large, fleshy tonsils; a bulbous or elongated uvula; and folds of excess tissue on the back wall of the throat. When these anatomic obstructions coexist, they are described as *crowding of the oropharynx.*

Nasal surgery such as septoplasty or turbinectomy is sometimes performed at the same time as UPPP, this combination of procedures referred to as *upper airway revision surgery.*

*Technique:* Uvulopalatopharyngoplasty is always performed under a general anesthetic. If present, the tonsils are removed, together with excess tissue around the tonsils. The surgeon then removes tissue from the edge of the soft palate to expand the airway, yet at the same time not removing too much so as to interfere with speech or swallowing. The edges of the incision are then sutured, stretching the back wall of the throat and expanding the pharyngeal airway.

*Postoperative care:* Patients are carefully monitored in the immediate postoperative period, sometimes in an intensive care unit. Those with severe sleep apnea or those who are extremely obese may require a temporary tracheostomy (described later in this chapter) prior to surgery, to protect their upper airway. For the same reason, nasal continuous positive airway pressure (nasal CPAP) is sometimes introduced during the first few postoperative days. If, however, any nasal surgery has been performed, surgical packing usually fills the nose, making the use of CPAP impossible.

There is always some swelling inside the throat. For this reason, elevation of the head, application of ice packs, intravenous cortisone and antibiotics all play a role in reducing this postoperative swelling. Patients will have an extremely sore throat for at least 10 days following this surgery, making swallowing very difficult. For this reason, they usually remain hospitalized for several days until the pain subsides and until they are able to swallow without too much difficulty.

It is important to note some of the side-effects of UPPP. Because throat tissue has been removed, the function of swallowing is altered; there may be some regurgitation of fluids through your nose. Similarly, your voice may take on a nasal quality. Fortunately, these effects are usually temporary; the functions of speech and swallowing usually return to normal once the postoperative swelling subsides and healing occurs. Unfortunately, a small percentage of patients may have a permanent change in their voice or some persistent nasal regurgitation.

*Results:* The success rate for eliminating snoring or substantially reducing it after UPPP is about 95 percent. However, surgeons still disagree on the exact criteria for surgical success of this operation for sleep apnea. When apnea is present, *complete* success is judged by the elimination of daytime tiredness and fatigue.

The debate regarding success rates following uvulopalatopharyngoplasty revolves around whether the

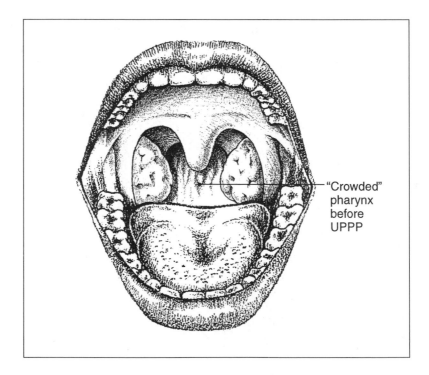

"Crowded" pharynx before UPPP

persistence of *any* symptoms of sleep apnea after surgery can qualify the procedure as being fully successful. In addition, some patients feel much better following surgery, their snoring disappears and they feel more energized during the day, yet overnight sleep studies show varying degrees of residual sleep apnea. To clarify this issue, therefore, a postoperative sleep study is always recommended for patients undergoing uvulopalatopharyngoplasty for sleep apnea.

*Surgical operation*: Punctate diathermy of the soft palate

*Definition:* An operation to produce scarring in the soft palate, stiffen it and lessen vibration. Developed in Great Britain and performed by a small number of surgeons, this procedure is, to my knowledge, not being done

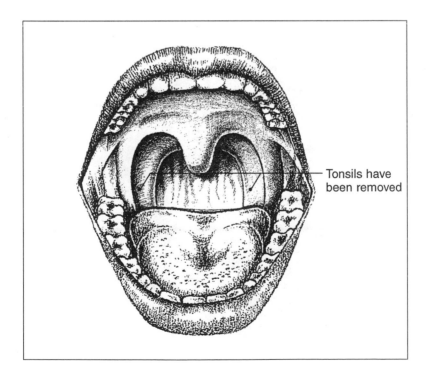

Tonsils have been removed

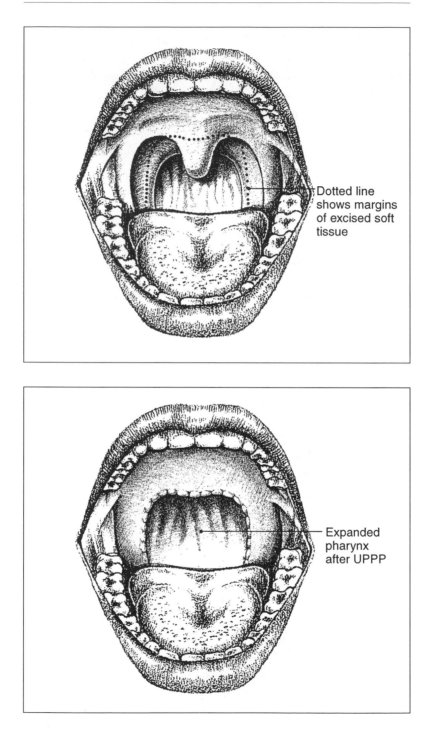

Dotted line shows margins of excised soft tissue

Expanded pharynx after UPPP

in the United States. Performed under a general anesthetic, the surgeon inserts an electrocautery needle into multiple areas on the soft palate, producing scar tissue within this structure.

*Postoperative care:* Patients experience a sore throat for approximately one week following this surgery, responding to pain medication, soothing gargles and a soft diet.

*Results:* According to Dr. Philip G. Bicknell, a British surgeon who has performed hundreds of these procedures, snoring can be eliminated in more than 80 percent of cases.

A more sophisticated version of punctate diathermy (which uses electrocautery) is now available, appearing to hold much promise for the treatment of snoring. Known as *Coblation*, this device is based on a bipolar design which converts fluid between the surgical instrument and the tissue to which it is applied into an ionized vapor layer, called *plasma*. Particles in this plasma layer accelerate towards the tissue with sufficient energy to break molecular bonds, resulting in cellular disintegration. Because this effect is confined to the surface layer of target tissue at temperatures of approximately 100° C, thermal damage to surrounding tissue is minimized. Coblation-treated tissue shows none of the charring and blanching, evident with the electrocautery. The potential result appears to be less discomfort with more rapid healing.

This office procedure is performed under local anesthetic, much the same as laser-assisted uvulopalatoplasty (LAUP) and Somnoplasty, techniques described in later chapters.

The coblation wand is introduced at several sites into the soft palate for short periods of 10 to 15 seconds, coagulating an area around the wand tip. Coblation is therefore a method of decreasing soft palate vibration by inducing stiffening and scarring of this structure.

In a small series, patients in Europe, treated by this method, yielded impressive results. Another clinical study to determine the efficacy of Coblation for snoring is currently underway in Portland, Oregon, conducted by this author.

### Surgery of the Hypopharynx

Symptoms of sleep apnea may persist for some patients who have had a UPPP operation. For these, surgeons have developed a series of more complex surgical procedures. Applying a surgical protocol developed by surgeons working with sleep disorders specialists at the Stanford School of Medicine Sleep Disorders Center, these more extensive procedures for severe sleep apnea are referred to as *phase 2 therapy*.

These surgeries are never done for snoring alone. Instead, they are restricted to a small percentage of patients—most of whom suffer from marked obesity—whose airway, even after UPPP, is still obstructed because of a recessed jaw or a large tongue intruding into the back of their throat. Some of these procedures include *partial glossectomy* (tongue reduction), *mandibular osteotomy with hyoid suspension* and *tongue advancement* (elevation of throat muscles and repositioning of the tongue) and *maxillary and mandibular advancement* (realignment of upper and lower jaws).

These surgeries are infrequently performed and are done by a relatively small number of highly specialized surgeons working in conjunction with sleep disorders centers. Should you be a candidate for such surgery, I recommend that you discuss the procedure in detail with your physician, recognizing that these operations are indicated only for incapacitating sleep apnea, when all other methods of treatment have been unsuccessful.

**Surgery on the Trachea**

*Surgical operation:* Tracheostomy

*Definition:* A surgical procedure for opening the trachea (windpipe) in order to bypass the upper airway.

*Indications:* Until the early 1980's, tracheostomy was the accepted surgical treatment—the only one available—for severe obstructive sleep apnea especially in obese patients, before the development of UPPP and surgery on the hypopharynx. Today, tracheostomy is rarely done as a primary procedure; it is never done for snoring alone. Instead, it may be an emergency measure for severely apneic patients with life-threatening cardiac arrhythmias or airway obstruction. In addition, tracheostomy to protect the airway may sometimes be required prior to performing UPPP in obese patients with severe forms of apnea. For similar reasons, this operation may also be done as an adjunct to hypopharyngeal surgeries.

*Postoperative care:* Tracheostomy requires intensive postoperative care. Accumulated secretions from the lungs have to be suctioned through the tracheostomy tube and inhaled air must be artificially humidified.

*Results:* A tracheostomy immediately relieves all the symptoms of sleep apnea. However, living with a tube in your throat presents serious difficulties. You have to cover the tube in order to speak; there are always increased secretions; there is an added tendency toward lung infections; and you are not permitted to swim. For these reasons, once the tracheostomy has bypassed your upper airway obstruction, surgeons today usually perform a subsequent operation, if possible, in an effort to overcome the obstruction, remove the tracheostomy tube and allow the patient to resume a normal life.

## Deciding on Surgery

Discuss any recommended surgery with your physician, keeping in mind that the preceding descriptions are not meant to be definitive but introductory—familiarizing you with some of the surgeries currently performed for snoring and sleep apnea. Ask your physician about his or her experience with these operations. Inquire about the exact nature of the procedure being performed, possible complications, length of time in the hospital, loss of time from work and any other questions relevant to your concerns. Of course, your questions should also deal with the cost of surgery and whether it will be covered by your insurance, recognizing that in addition to your surgeon's fee there will be other expenses—the hospital's charges and the anesthesiologist's fees.

The decision to undergo surgery should not be taken lightly. As with any other major decision, it should be made *only* after you have obtained a body of well-balanced information on the subject.

# Chapter 9

# Snore Wars: Laser Your ZZZZ Away

As recently as 1990, a French surgeon, Dr. Yves-Victor Kamami, introduced a revolutionary technique to treat snoring with a laser. Reporting his results in the European medical literature, Dr. Kamami claimed a success rate of more than 85 percent. This innovative surgeon called his procedure *laser vaporization of the palatopharynx* (LVPP), in which he reshaped and shortened the uvula and soft palate.

Laser surgery for snoring, introduced into the United States in 1992 by Dr. Jack Coleman, in Nashville and Dr. Yosef Krespi, in New York, is rapidly gaining popularity with ear, nose and throat specialists throughout the country. Referred to as *laser-assisted uvulopalatoplasty* (LAUP) in the U.S., this procedure has become widely accepted by patients as a quick, safe and effective snoring remedy.

199

# How a Laser Works

Before discussing this new laser surgery and how suitable candidates are chosen for treatment, we need to explain what a laser is and how it works.

Somehow, the word *laser* conjures up images of powerful beings from another planet, locked in mortal combat with light swords giving out deadly rays. In fact, a laser is essentially a device producing very concentrated beams of light, much like a powerful magnifying glass focusing the sun's rays on one small spot.

Light is a combined electric and magnetic wave, traveling through space. Any light wave has a characteristic wavelength, defined as the distance between adjacent crests of that wave. The human eye interprets different wavelengths of light as different colors. Red light, for example, has a longer wavelength than blue light.

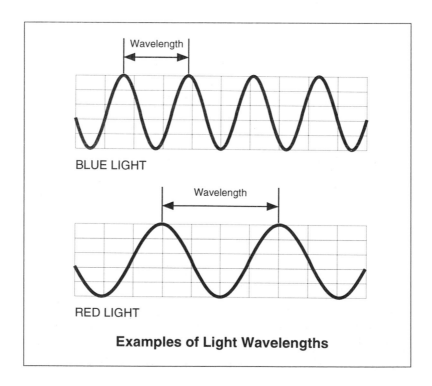

BLUE LIGHT

RED LIGHT

**Examples of Light Wavelengths**

Ordinary sources of light such as the sun or an electric light bulb produce a wide range of wavelengths, emitted in all directions. When sunlight is focused on one spot, for example, by using a magnifying glass outdoors, the sun's rays become concentrated, producing heat. This process can be used to light a fire or burn holes in a piece of wood. The concept of a laser, therefore, is to produce a powerful source of energy by focusing *all* of the rays emanating from a light source onto one small area. In fact, even a small laser, at close range, produces light much brighter than the sun.

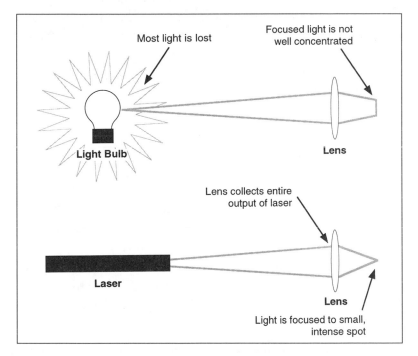

The word *laser* stands for *light amplification by stimulated emission of radiation*. Laser light energy results from electrically exciting a gas, such as carbon dioxide. Rapidly moving gas particles shed off tiny wavelets of light, called *photons*. These photons are bounced back and forth between mirrors in a laser tube, stimulating other light particles into motion. When released, these parallel light beams are amplified, yielding high levels of heat energy. Used as a surgical tool, laser light is focused on a small area of the body, selectively vaporizing it.

Modern day lasers, therefore, are extremely useful surgical instruments, allowing safe and accurate excision or removal of tissue, virtually without bleeding, and producing minimal damage to surrounding structures.

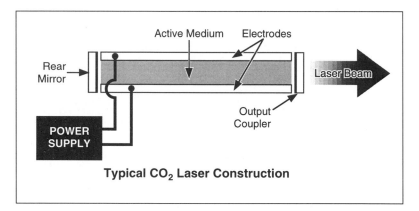

**Typical $CO_2$ Laser Construction**

## Who Can Benefit From Laser Surgery?

Snorers for whom conservative methods of treatment have been unsuccessful, and whose snoring continues unabated, are candidates for *laser-assisted uvulopalatoplasty* (LAUP). Obviously, a careful medical evaluation is essential prior to considering any surgery, including LAUP. This evaluation should include a detailed sleep history, review of past medical problems, a complete examination of the upper airway by an ear, nose and throat specialist, and an overnight sleep study, if deemed appropriate.

Snoring patients should all be given the opportunity of conservative treatment, including modification of lifestyle, weight control, positional therapy and treatment of nasal congestion. These methods are discussed in the previous chapter. For those frustrated snorers, whose honking continues to disrupt their households, the following are candidates for LAUP:

♦ Socially disruptive snorers, without symptoms of sleep apnea, who have failed conservative methods of treatment.

♦ Severe snorers with symptoms of daytime tiredness despite a normal overnight sleep study. This group of patients would include those diagnosed with the *upper airway resistance syndrome*, discussed in a previous chapter.

♦ Snorers with confirmed sleep apnea of a mild or moderate degree, in whom careful evaluation shows their obstruction to be isolated to the uvula and soft palate. The new procedure of LAUP, introduced here as *site-specific surgery*, should be considered only after patients in this category have been offered nasal CPAP and are either unable or unwilling to tolerate this form of treatment.

♦ Some patients who have undergone uvulopalato-pharyngoplasty (UPPP) in the past and are now having recurrence of snoring from sagging throat tissues.

♦ Certain sleep apnea patients, currently using CPAP, require high opening pressures to control their apnea. Laser reduction of their throat tissues, by expanding their pharyngeal airway, can make CPAP treatment more tolerable.

## Who Are Not Candidates for LAUP?

Laser-assisted uvulopalatoplasty was designed ostensibly to remove excess uvular and soft palate tissue, while simultaneously firming these structures. Snorers, therefore, with severe nasal obstruction, from any cause, should have this corrected before considering LAUP. The laser can now be used to shrink swollen nasal tissues in those who have not gained relief from decongestants, nasal sprays or allergy shots.

Similarly, those with large tonsils or a prominent tongue will not have their problem corrected by surgery on the palate. Large tonsils, however, can be treated by laser. With a technique known as *laser tonsillar cryptolysis*, the tonsil surface is abraded, under local anesthetic, in repeated sessions. This progressively reduces the size of the tonsils. Although said to be safer than conventional tonsillectomy, by avoiding a general anesthetic, serial laser tonsillar cryptolysis is nevertheless a somewhat painful and time-consuming procedure.

Patients with an uncontrollable gag reflex may have difficulty tolerating laser surgery on their throat under local anesthetic. In my experience, however, with careful explanation, relaxation and thorough application of topical anesthetic, a gag reflex does not usually present an obstacle to successful laser surgery. Trismus (inability to fully open the mouth) may limit adequate access to the uvula and soft palate.

Because any surgery on the palate can change the voice, professional singers, actors, or wind-instrument players should consider LAUP with caution. Similarly, those who speak languages which use the soft palate extensively, such as Arabic, Russian, Hebrew or Farsi may have some pronunciation difficulties after surgery.

Perhaps the greatest controversy surrounding laser-assisted uvulopalatoplasty, inviting disfavor from some sleep disorders specialists, is the claim, in some medical circles, that LAUP can replace traditional uvulopalato-pharyngoplasty. LAUP is essentially a safe yet conservative surgery, not indicated in the presence of pharyngeal crowding or with sleep apnea of any severity.

# How Is LAUP Performed?

Laser-assisted uvulopalatoplasty is performed in an office or clinic setting. Patients are usually instructed not to eat or drink on the day of their surgery.

The patient sits in an upright chair, and after explaining details of the laser procedure, the surgeon numbs the throat with anesthetic spray. A small amount of local anesthetic solution is then injected, much like preparation for a dental filling.

Following a standard protocol for laser safety, the surgeon wears goggles, mask and gloves. All personnel in the room, including the patient, wear protective eyeglasses or goggles.

Laser vaporization of the throat begins by creating "gothic arches" in the soft palate on either side of the uvula. Next, the uvula is shortened and reshaped. Each of these steps is performed with a carbon dioxide laser handpiece called a *backstop*, which protects surrounding structures from stray laser rays.

After a soothing mouth-rinse the patient leaves the office with instructions regarding diet, medication, mouth care and physical activity.

A sore throat will inevitably follow LAUP surgery. This discomfort, which is often accompanied by ear pain, lasts from one to two weeks, and is usually controlled by the judicious use of pain medication, local anesthetic mouthwashes and gargles. The patient should avoid hot foods or those with a high acid content such as citrus or tropical fruits.

Healing takes place over the next few weeks. In this process of healing, scar tissue develops around the uvula and soft palate, shortening and stiffening these structures, enhancing the desired effect to resolve snoring.

Although laser-assisted uvulopalatoplasty appears to be a safe procedure with minimal complications, some side-effects may include a dry mouth, painful ears and a temporary change in voice quality. In addition, although highly unlikely, some bleeding or infection may occur.

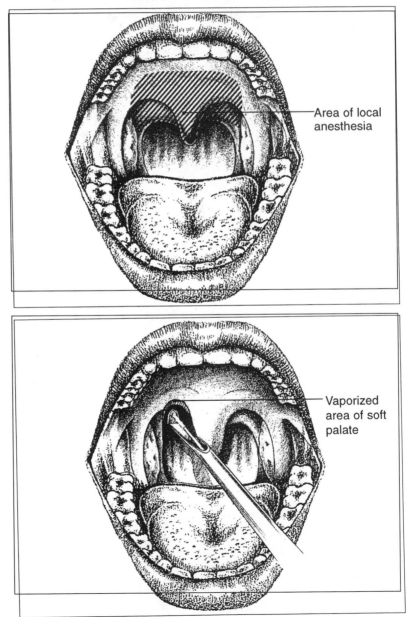

Area of local anesthesia

Vaporized area of soft palate

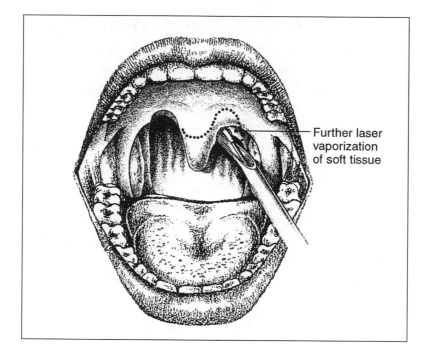

Further laser
vaporization
of soft tissue

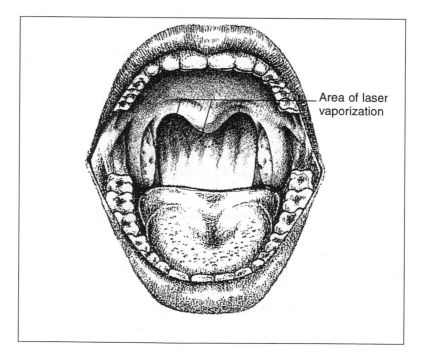

Area of laser
vaporization

## Does LAUP Have to be Repeated?

In the original description of LAUP, Dr. Kamami described a series of laser surgeries, from three to five sessions, spaced approximately one month apart. Many U.S. surgeons follow a similar technique of multiple surgeries.

However, as our experience with LAUP evolves, some surgeons now attempt to complete laser resection of the uvula and soft palate in *one* session. This technique is known as *one-stage laser palatal reconstruction*. Even with this more radical approach, however, approximately ten percent of patients will require a second laser surgery; a very small percentage will need more than two procedures.

## Results of LAUP

Laser surgery on the uvula and palate for snoring has been performed for less than five years. Consequently, early results, although promising, do not necessarily reflect long-term outcome.

In one of the earliest papers by Yosef Krespi, M.D., describing LAUP results in 280 patients, 84 percent were cured of their snoring; 7 percent reported some improvement; the remaining 9 percent were not helped or discontinued treatment.

In my own experience of having performed LAUP on more than 3,000 patients, results have been very similar—an overall success rate (complete cessation of snoring or reduction to tolerable volumes) of 93 percent.

Patients diagnosed with the *upper airway resistance syndrome* (discussed in an earlier chapter) report similar good results with their snoring; daytime sleepiness improves in more than 90 percent of cases.

The exact role of LAUP in the treatment of sleep apnea, however, remains somewhat uncertain. To date, only a few reports on LAUP results have appeared in the medical literature.

Regina Walker, M.D., of Loyola University, in one of the first published papers on this subject, describes her results of postoperative sleep studies after laser surgery. Thirty-three patients with sleep apnea underwent overnight sleep testing after their LAUP surgery. Forty-eight percent of these had a postoperative respiratory disturbance index (RDI) of less than 10; 64 percent showed a reduction in their preoperative RDI by 50 percent or more. The conclusion to be drawn, even at this early stage, in a small series of patients, is that in selected cases with relatively mild sleep apnea, the overall success rates of LAUP are very similar to those of conventional UPPP surgery.

After a fanfare of publicity from the media and some laser companies heralding the introduction of laser surgery for snoring into the United States, official organizations such as the American Sleep Disorders Association (ASDA) were called upon to clarify issues of indications, risks and potential complications of LAUP.

After assembling a group of medical specialists, the ASDA, through their Standards of Practice Committee, in December 1994, issued the following recommendations:

- Objective data do not exist in peer-reviewed medical journals regarding the efficacy of LAUP for sleep-related breathing disorders.
  [Note: This statement is now inaccurate.]

- Surgical candidates for LAUP should undergo thorough preoperative clinical evaluation. This should include an objective measure of respiration when sleep apnea is suspected.

- Patients should be informed that the risks, benefits and complications of LAUP have not yet been fully established.

- Patients undergoing LAUP for the treatment of snoring should be informed that underlying sleep apnea

may be masked by this treatment. They should therefore be medically evaluated on a regular basis.

These recommendations have inevitably led to some
confusion among both patients and physicians. As a result, sleep disorders specialists have been somewhat reluctant to recommend LAUP, whereas otolaryngologists
continue to be enthused by its good results and low com-
plication rate.

The time is ripe for better communication between di-
verse specialties involved in the treatment of sleep-induced
breathing disorders. Sleep disorders specialists, drawn from
the disciplines of pulmonology and neurology will often
favor conservative, non-invasive treatments; surgeons, who
are people of action, look for ready surgical solutions to
clinical problems.

# Chapter 10

# Stay Tuned:

## Radiofrequency Applications for Snoring and Sleep Apnea

As recently as 1997, the U.S. Food and Drug Administration cleared the use of a radiofrequency electrical device, applied briefly to the soft palate as a treatment for habitual snoring. This innovative technique, known as the *Somnoplasty®* procedure, is now being effectively utilized as a safe treatment for offensive snoring throughout the United States and, in fact, in many parts of the world. This technique has also now been cleared by the FDA (1998) for the treatment of obstructive sleep apnea.

To understand how this sophisticated new system works, we need to briefly review the principles of high-frequency electrical current, used as a surgical tool. Any living tissue comprises billions of cells which act as electrical conductors due to their chemical composition. The tiny molecules in every cell are continually jiggling and bouncing, turning and twisting around each other, glued together by an electrochemical bond.

211

When we introduce electrical energy into any tissue, the movement of the molecules increases, expanding the distance between each of these minute structures and loosening the bonds holding them together. From the practical point of view, this process produces heat, which diffuses throughout the material exposed to high-frequency current. In general terms, this principle is applied in households today with the modern microwave oven.

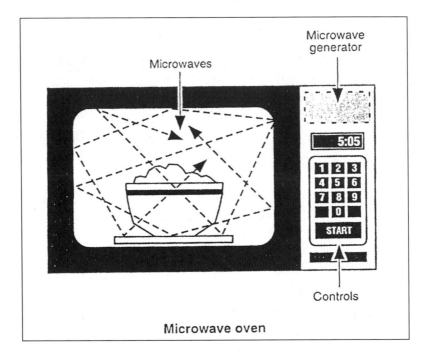

**Microwave oven**

Electrosurgical effects on living tissues are possible with electrical currents of any frequency between 100,000 and four million cycles per second. However, most surgical generators produce currents in the order of 500,000 cycles per second, the same range as the electromagnetic radiation of radio waves. For this reason, the electrical energy used in surgery is called *radiofrequency current*. Specifically, the Somnoplasty system utilizes a frequency of 465 KiloHertz (465,000 cycles per second).

The manner in which electrosurgical current is applied determines the subsequent clinical response. At low power, the effects are essentially heating and coagulation of tissue; at higher power, a spark produces a cutting effect. Irrespective of the specific technique, conversion of high-frequency electrical energy into heat in any tissue is called *surgical diathermy* (derived from the Greek *dia* = through; *therme* = heat). Radiofrequency tissue volume reduction is therefore a minimally invasive method by which a subsurface targeted area is selectively heated, precisely controlled by a temperature monitor, known as a *thermocouple*.

Admittedly, the concept of producing surgical destruction of tissue with electrical current is not a new one. Soon after the beginning of the twentieth century, Dr. Beaunis applied electrodes to the brains of experimental animals. Similar experiments were conducted during the next few decades by Doctors Golsinger, Horsley and Clarke. Interestingly, the interactions of radiofrequency currents on tissue began with the early ham radio operators, who experienced the unpleasant effects of touching the wrong parts of their transmitters! Applying these principles, Dr. Harvey Cushing, the famous Harvard neurosurgeon, studied the use of radiofrequency power for surgical cutting and coagulating.

The first commercially available radiofrequency generators were built in the early 1950's by Drs. Aranow and Cosman, and have, for many years, been applied in neurosurgery. In recent years, a similar technique has been introduced in urology for the treatment of enlarged prostate glands.

As you can now understand, when low levels of high-frequency energy are applied to the soft palate for the treatment of snoring, current flows into the surrounding tissues. This in turn causes molecular friction, generating heat. The heated area, which ultimately shrinks by a de-

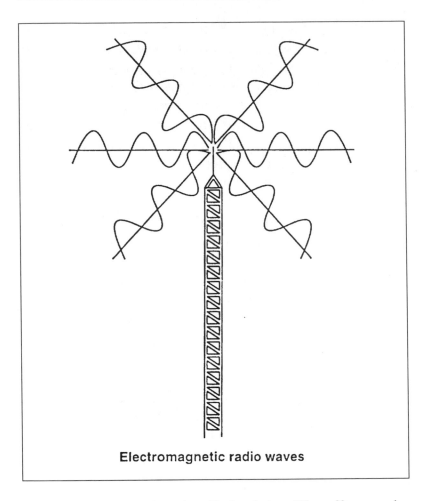

**Electromagnetic radio waves**

layed scarring reaction, is called a *lesion*. The effect on the soft palate, therefore, is to shrink and tighten this structure, reducing its vibration, with a correspondingly beneficial effect on snoring.

Immediately after a Somnoplasty procedure, there is a slight amount of swelling in the soft palate; and then, over the following few days, a scarring reaction begins, shrinking and firming this treated area. This reaction is usually complete after seven or eight weeks, by which time scar tissue has formed. This new tissue has less volume than the normal structure. In fact, experimental surgery in laboratory animals has shown a volume reduction of at least 25% after radiofrequency thermal ablation. These results have now been duplicated in human subjects.

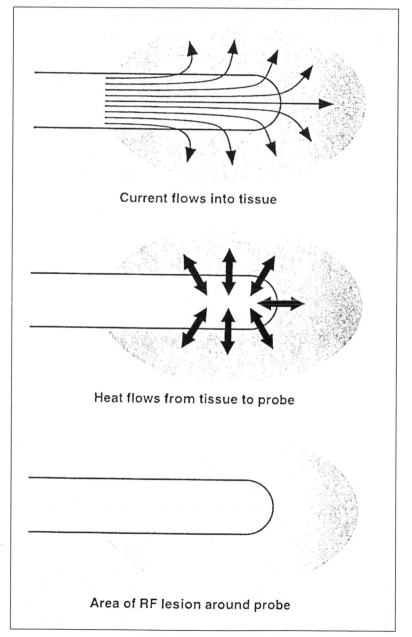

Current flows into tissue

Heat flows from tissue to probe

Area of RF lesion around probe

## Who Can Benefit from Radiofrequency Treatment?

Any snorer whose noisy habits have become a source of constant irritation to their bedroom partner and in whom conservative methods of treatment have failed to produce any realistic relief, is a candidate for the Somnoplasty treatment.

With the same careful approach used before contemplating conventional or laser surgery, a complete medical evaluation is recommended prior to considering radiofrequency therapy. This should include a detailed sleep history, review of past medical problems and a complete examination of the upper airway by an ear, nose and throat specialist. An overnight sleep study is not necessarily recommended as an essential preliminary to performing Somnoplasty procedures. However, if any symptoms or signs of obstructive sleep apnea are present, polysomnography may be deemed appropriate by the treating physician. This overnight sleep test is discussed in an earlier chapter.

Socially disruptive snorers seeking medical help should be given the opportunity of pursuing conservative treatment, which includes weight-control, positional therapy and the treatment of nasal congestion, methods covered in detail in previous chapters. Recognizing that radiofrequency thermal ablation to reduce tissue volume is a relatively new technique, representing a departure from other methods of treatment for snoring, sleep apnea and nasal congestion, indications for the Somnoplasty procedure are constantly being refined. At this time, candidates for this procedure are:

♦ Socially disruptive snorers, without symptoms of sleep apnea, who have failed to respond to conservative methods of treatment.

- Severe snorers with symptoms of daytime tiredness, despite a normal overnight sleep study. This group includes those diagnosed with the *upper airway resistance syndrome*, discussed in a previous chapter. It is essential, however, that other causes of excess daytime sleepiness be excluded by appropriate medical testing.

- Some patients who have undergone either conventional surgery (UPPP) or laser surgery (LAUP) and are now having recurrence of snoring from sagging soft palate tissues. At this time, a relatively small number of patients in this category have been treated with the Somnoplasty procedure; additional clinical studies are presently being conducted in medical centers around the U.S.A.

- Similarly, those with residual features of obstructive sleep apnea (to a mild or moderate degree) despite undergoing upper airway expansion surgery. In this group, a prominent tongue base is often the underlying cause for persistent OSA symptoms. The FDA have recently given clearance for the Somnoplasty system to reduce tongue tissue volume, overcoming the airway obstruction.

- Conceivably, tongue base volume reduction will become a valuable adjunct to those patients using continuous positive airway pressure (CPAP) making their long-term treatment more acceptable and effective.

## Who Are Not Candidates for Radiofrequency Treatment?

The Somnoplasty procedure was developed to tighten and shrink excess soft palate tissue. Loud snorers, therefore, who experience severe nasal obstruction should have this resolved before considering radiofrequency therapy. This may involve medical, immunological or surgical treatment.

Interestingly, FDA clearance was recently granted for radiofrequency ablation to shrink swollen nasal tissues.

Patients whose pharyngeal airways are obstructed by large tonsils are currently not candidates for the Somnoplasty procedure. However, experimental studies are currently underway to reduce the tissue bulk of enlarged tonsils with this technique.

In an earlier chapter, we alluded to the valuable contributions of a Japanese physician, Dr. Ikematsu, who developed a system *(mesopharyngometry)* for measuring the anatomical variants of the upper airway, correlating these observations with degrees of snoring. Certain anatomical features, described by Dr. Ikematsu (such as an elongated uvula or prominent tonsillar pillars), may mitigate against radiofrequency treatment alone. In these situations, Somnoplasty treatments, combined with another form of treatment (such as laser surgery) may successfully account for more complete snoring control.

Some patients with a hyperactive gag reflex may have some difficulty tolerating the electrodes applied to their palates. However, with suitable topical anesthetic and sedation (where appropriate), a prominent gag reflex should not present any obstacle to successful treatment. Severe trismus (inability to fully open the mouth) may, however, limit adequate exposure.

The soft palate is used to produce certain speech sounds. Modifying the shape of this structure, therefore, may affect vocal quality, albeit in a subtle way. Actors, professional singers or wind-instrument players should recognize the remote possibility of vocal change with this form of treatment. Although these side-effects have not been reported, patients who speak languages using the soft palate extensively (eg. French, German, Hebrew, Farsi) should consider the possibility of vocal side-effects following radiofrequency treatment.

Without doubt, the Somnoplasty procedure will generate, among its greatest number of detractors, some sleep disorders specialists who feel that this procedure may possibly disguise some patients with underlying severe obstructive sleep apnea. A similar objection was raised rather vigorously, several years ago, when laser surgery was introduced for the treatment of snoring. However, the medical literature now supports evidence that laser surgery *does*, in fact, have a place in the treatment of sleep apnea. Similarly, current research demonstrates that radiofrequency tissue volume reduction also plays a significant contributory role.

## How is RFTVR performed?

Radiofrequency tissue volume reduction (**RFTVR**) for snoring is essentially a brief office procedure. There are no preliminary blood tests, x-rays, or preoperative medications required.

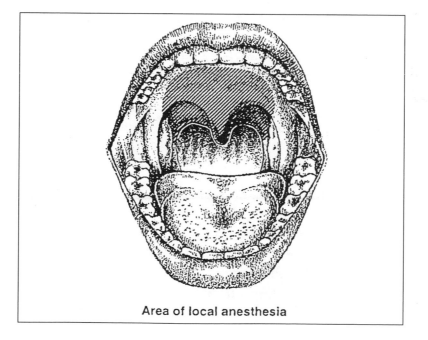

Area of local anesthesia

After a thorough explanation of the procedure to be performed, the patient completes the appropriate paperwork, giving informed consent. With the patient sitting upright, the surgeon numbs their throat with anesthetic spray, followed by an injection of local anesthetic solution into the soft palate. Essentially, the preparation for this procedure is much the same as for laser-assisted uvulopalatoplasty. When tongue-base reduction is performed, topical and local anesthetic is introduced into the back of the tongue.

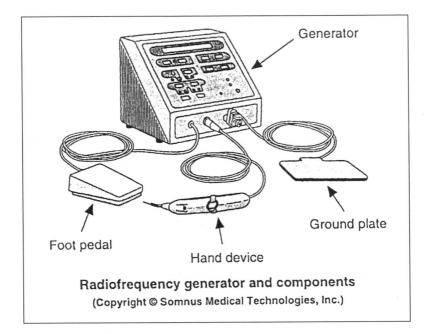

Generator

Foot pedal

Hand device

Ground plate

**Radiofrequency generator and components**
(Copyright © Somnus Medical Technologies, Inc.)

A self-adhesive ground pad is placed directly onto the patient's skin, usually on their back. This completes an electrical circuit when the electrode is introduced into the palate. After measuring the contour of the patient's palate, the physician delicately bends the needle electrode to match this shape, inserting it into the soft palate above the uvula. The assistant then activates the radiofrequency control unit (with a foot-pedal), progressively increasing the amount of energy delivered through the electrode. This aspect of the procedure is usually done in less than 15 minutes, during which time the patient experiences no discomfort. Following completion of a Somnoplasty treatment session, the electrode is withdrawn and the patient leaves the office with instructions regarding diet, medication and mouth care.

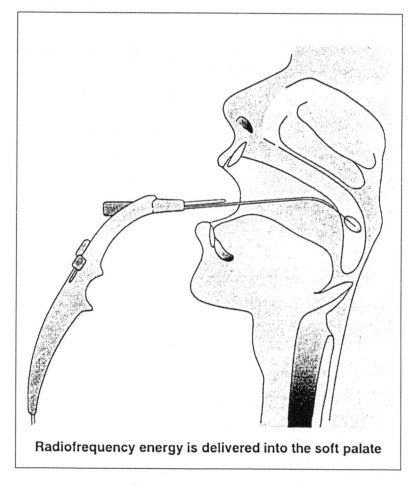

**Radiofrequency energy is delivered into the soft palate**

There is usually minimal discomfort following the Somnoplasty procedure. Most patients report a slight degree of irritation or swelling in their mouths, lasting no more than a day or two. Blistering in the mucus membranes occasionally occurs. This mild discomfort can usually be controlled by over-the-counter analgesics and mouthwashes. Very hot foods, or those with a high acid content (such as citrus or tropical fruits) should be avoided for the first few days, after which time patients can resume their regular diets.

The healing reaction in the palate is usually complete by six to eight weeks. During this time, scarring develops within the muscles of the soft palate, shrinking and stiffening this structure, enhancing the desired effect to resolve snoring.

Tongue volume reduction is performed in a similar fashion. After suitable local anesthesia, a specially designed pre-formed electrode is gently introduced into several areas around the tongue base, to a depth of several centimeters. Because of the increased tongue tissue volume (compared with the soft palate), several treatments are usually required to produce a successful outcome.

Additionally, we recommend a period of monitoring and close observation (usually over 24 hours) following the initial tongue base treatment in case any reactive swelling causes upper airway obstruction. To date, such obstructive breathing problems have not been encountered following treatment.

Postoperative care for the tongue base Somnoplasty procedure includes pain control, treatment of any swelling with antibiotics or cortisone (at the surgeon's discretion), as well as CPAP, until the tongue swelling subsides. (See CPAP, chapter 8.)

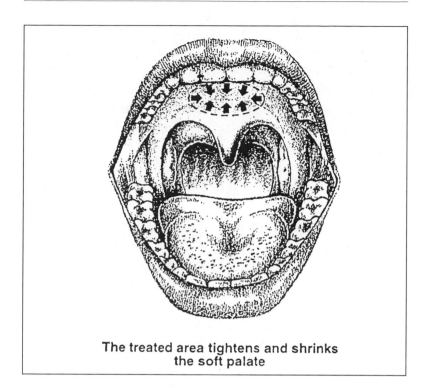

**The treated area tightens and shrinks
the soft palate**

## Results of the Somnoplasty Procedure

Radiofrequency thermal ablation of the soft palate for snoring has been available for a relatively short time. As stated, FDA clearance was only granted in mid-1997, yet early reports from pilot clinical studies are extremely promising. These preliminary results, however, do not necessarily reflect long-term success. For the record, clearance by the Food and Drug Administration is provided only after animal and human studies have satisfactorily proven that a device is safe and efficacious for its designated purpose.

In one of the early papers by Nelson Powell, M.D. and Robert Riley, M.D., describing radiofrequency treatment results in 23 patients, snoring was satisfactorily resolved in the majority of patients in this study. These snorers each received from one to three treatment applications; there were few side-effects and complications in this group; and patients were able to resume a regular diet and full physical activities immediately after treatment.

Clinical investigators at the University of Maryland and Vanderbilt University, Nashville, report similarly beneficial results (close to 80 percent success) and an absence of complications in their patients undergoing the Somnoplasty treatment. At the time of this writing, my own experience with radiofrequency thermal ablation has been uniformly positive, confirming its place as a safe, effective and virtually painless treatment for snoring.

A published clinical study on the outcome of the Somnoplasty procedure for sleep apnea by Nelson Powell, M.D. compared the respiratory disturbance index (RDI) before and after treatment. Sleep studies on 16 patients, before and after treatment, showed a significant improvement in the number of apneic episodes during sleep. Additionally, there was an impressive reduction in daytime sleepiness and fatigue following treatment.

## Open Your Mind and Say "Ahhh"

We currently live in an age of remarkable technological progress. Without realizing it, the microchip, that miraculous workhorse at the heart of every computer, is pressed into service whenever we use our credit cards, fax a letter or turn on our VCR.

Every arena of human endeavor has been affected by this explosion of knowledge, none more so than the field of modern healthcare. As physicians, it is sometimes difficult to adapt to the sweeping changes which influence the way we practice. Sadly, it is all too easy to turn a blind eye to progress, clinging to older, more traditional methods of clinical investigation and treatment.

Musing over the somewhat negative and even hostile attitudes of some physician colleagues toward the newer, sophisticated techniques described in these closing chapters, I recall the noble words of Howard Roark, Ayn Rand's architect hero in *The Fountainhead*:

> Thousands of years ago, the first man discovered how to make fire. Considered an evildoer, he was probably burned at the stake with the fire he had taught his brothers to light. But thereafter, men had fire for warmth, to cook food, to light their caves . . .

> Centuries later, the first man invented the wheel. Without doubt, he was regarded as a transgressor, venturing into forbidden territory. But thereafter, men could travel past any horizon. The inventor had left them a gift they had not conceived which opened the roads of the world. . .

> Down the ages, many of those who had the courage to take first steps, venturing into the unknown, were hated; every new idea opposed. But these early men, armed with little more than their talent and vision, forged ahead. They fought, they suffered, they paid. But they ultimately triumphed by making a better world for their brothers, using the products of their minds. . .

It is often a challenge for physicians to embrace revolutionary new concepts of diagnosis and treatment, incorporating them into their professional lives. Nevertheless, I feel that we are obligated to offer our patients appropriate choice morsels from this smorgasbord of contemporary technological wizardry, hopefully introduced with judgement and applied with skill.

I do not regard the high-tech innovations described in these final chapters as either a miracle or a panacea. They do, however, represent significant milestones of modern medical progress and powerful weapons against snoring. . . the night's worst nuisance and its darker, more ominous side. . . obstructive sleep apnea.

# Chapter 11

# Here's to Quiet Nights from Now On:

## Future Directions in
## Sleep Apnea Research

Approximately 40 million Americans suffer from chronic disorders of sleep and wakefulness, such as *sleep apnea, narcolepsy,* and *the insomnias.* The majority of those affected remain undiagnosed and untreated. An additional 20 to 30 million individuals experience intermittent sleep-related problems. Moreover, at any given time, many millions of others obtain inadequate sleep because of demanding work schedules and other lifestyle factors.

The consequences of sleep disorders, sleep deprivation and sleepiness are enormous. They include reduced productivity, lower mental performance, the increased likelihood of accidents, a higher morbidity/mortality risk and a decreased quality of life. Further, the consequences span all aspects of modern society: Manufacturing, energy production, transportation, government, military, health care, education, family and social life.

While the Exxon Valdez is a particularly flagrant example of the negative consequences of excessive sleepiness, it is not an isolated event. Sleep disorders can affect us all at some point in our lives. The Department of Transportation estimates that 200,000 reported automobile accidents each year may be sleep-related. Twenty percent of *all* drivers have fallen asleep behind the wheel on at least one occasion. One survey of 1,500 drivers found that 69 percent had experienced drowsiness while driving. Fatigue and excess sleepiness were implicated in a greater number of heavy truck fatalities than were alcohol and other drugs of abuse. In fact, the most frequently cited cause of mass transportation accidents is fatigue, accounting for nearly one-third of all heavy-trucking driver fatalities.

At this moment, sleep-deprived individuals are operating millions of motor vehicles, including high-tonnage trucks. They are operating trains, airplanes and ships of all kinds. They are in responsible decision-making positions, monitoring nuclear power plants and space missions, controlling air traffic and staffing strategic military installations. The cost to the individual is enormous; the potential for catastrophe is great.

Despite their wide-ranging impact on our society, sleep-related problems are not yet recognized as a public health issue. Americans sadly lack basic information about sleep and sleep disorders. Health care professionals receive minimal training in this area. Both the public and private sectors largely disregard the impact of sleep on productivity and safety. Thus, as a whole, American society fails to recognize and attend effectively to sleep-related issues.

The National Commission on Sleep Disorders Research, mandated by Congress in section 162 of Public Law 100-607, was appointed by the Secretary of the Department of Health and Human Services in early 1989. This panel's charge was to conduct a comprehensive study of sleep disorders with a view to a long-range plan for organizing national resources, dealing effectively with sleep disorders research and medicine. The Commission's members included scientists, physicians and other health care professionals. Also on this panel were concerned members of the general public (including one with personal or family experience with sleep disorders), and personnel from the National Institutes of Health, involved with sleep disorders.

The Commission first met in 1990, holding public hearings in eight cities. The first hearing was held in Washington, D.C., before a standing-room only audience. Those in attendance heard witness after witness describe the devastating impact of sleep disorders and sleep deprivation on their own lives.

Initially, the Commission was surprised and somewhat daunted by the sheer number and diversity of the problems it encountered. It therefore focused its mandate on a few carefully stated and presumably achievable goals.

The following are recommendations by the National Commission on Sleep Disorders Research for immediate implementation to ensure the greatest benefit at the smallest cost:

**Recommendation 1: Establish a National Center.**
The commissioners unanimously agreed that the best possible mechanism to address the urgent needs of American society would be a national center within the National Institutes of Health. The Commission recommended that Congress authorize sufficient funds to support a national center for research and education on sleep and sleep disorders.

**A National Center for Sleep Disorders Research**
In June 1993, President Bill Clinton signed Public Law
103-43, creating the National Center for Sleep Disorders
Research, within the National Institutes of Health. This
research center was established to conduct and support
research, scientist training , dissemination of health information and other activities on sleep disorders and related
concerns. The Commission recommended that $16.4 mil-
lion be appropriated to establish this center.

**Recommendation 2: Strengthen ongoing programs.**
The Commission recommended that Federal support for
basic, clinical, and prevention research on sleep and sleep
disorders be expanded. This panel recommended an immediate increase of $55.8 million above existing levels to
support this enhanced research effort.

**Recommendation 3: Accountability in all Federal
agencies.**
The Commission recommended the establishment of specifically identified offices on sleep and sleep disorders within
all Federal departments and agencies. To support the establishment of these offices, the Commission recommended
an annual appropriation of $1.1 million.

**Recommendation 4: Training and career development.**
The Commission identified a serious absence of career and
training opportunities for young investigators interested
in the field of sleep and its disorders. Recognizing that research is essentially dedicated to better understanding and
treatment of sleep disorders, the Commission recommended that substantially increased levels of Federal support be directed to all NIH and relevant government agencies specifically for sleep disorder research training and career development opportunities. They recommended an

immediate increase in research training and career development funds of $2.5 million over existing levels.

**Recommendation 5: Education of health professionals.**
The Commission recommended that Congress encourage and support a broader awareness and training in sleep and sleep disorders, spanning the full range of health care professionals, particularly at the primary care level. They recommended an annual appropriation of $4 million to support these activities.

**Recommendation 6: An Educated America.**
The Commission recommended that a major public awareness/ education campaign about sleep and sleep disorders be undertaken immediately by the Federal government. To support this important project, the Commission recommended an additional annual appropriation of $3.25 million.

Clearly, more research is needed into sleep apnea, a condition which we now know affects many millions of people. We need more information on its prevalence; our current data is inaccurate, tending to underestimate this problem.

Although we recognize the potentially dangerous medical side-effects of sleep apnea, we have yet to determine the levels of severity which truly put any patient at risk.

Because of the vast numbers affected, the cost of so many complete sleep studies is staggering. Despite the negative economic effects of sleep apnea going undiagnosed and untreated, some medical insurance companies, in this new era of managed health care, remain somewhat reluctant to cover these services. There is, therefore, a desperate need for an effective, accurate and affordable screening test for sleep apnea.

The *respiratory disturbance index*, the basic yardstick by which we measure sleep apnea, may be less than practical; research into the correlation between apnea and EEG arousals may, in the future, introduce a new paradigm by which this condition is assessed.

Nasal continuous positive airway pressure, while remaining the cornerstone of non-invasive treatment, requires more refinement in order to increase long-term compliance. A new generation of interactive CPAP units, responding to the patient's individual breathing demands, offers much promise.

Specific indications for each surgical procedure need to be standardized, based on a *site-specific* approach. By the same token, reporting criteria and postoperative outcome studies will enhance our understanding of sleep apnea and improve treatment results.

Sleep-disorders specialists and otolaryngologists need to communicate more effectively, pooling their combined expertise for the patients' benefit. Primary care physicians *must* consider sleep habits in all their patient consultations, familiarizing themselves with commonly encountered sleep disorders in children and adults.

We have come a long way together in our discussion of snoring and sleep apnea. I hope that by now this book has provided you with the confidence that snoring need no longer intrude on your life and your relationships. In addition, sleep apnea sufferers can now readily turn to widely available resources for diagnosis and treatment.

It is my wish that your efforts in pursuit of a cure will bring vigor to your days and silence to your nights. In the words of David Frishberg, a well-known songwriter and jazz entertainer:

I don't need no vitamins or tonics
Or hormones off some monkey in the trees
I don't need no high or low colonics
Or jelly from royal honeybees
I got to get me some ZZZZ

I don't need no Turkish bath or sauna
I don't want no pills from no M.D.s
I could stay awake but I don't wanna
'Cause I'd be walking around on my knees
I got to get me some ZZZZ

I don't need no heavy conversation
Ain't got wind enough to shoot the breeze
I don't need no free association
With some Beverly Hills Viennese
I got to get me some ZZZZ

I don't want no whiskey or no highballs
I don't need no headaches or D.T.'s
Just dig these satchels underneath my eyeballs
Now if I'm going to get rid of these
I better get me some ZZZZ

# G-O-O-O-D NIGHT!

# Appendix I

# Sleep Disorders Associations, Organizations & Support Groups

**American Sleep Apnea Association**
2025 Pennsylvania Ave., N.W.
Suite 905
Washington, D.C. 20006
(202) 293-3650
Fax (202) 293-3656
Purpose: To educate the public about sleep apnea and reduce disability associated with sleep apnea and related breathing disorders during sleep.

**American Sleep Disorders Association**
1610 14th Street NW, Ste.300
Rochester, MN 55901
(507) 287-6006
Fax (507) 287-6008
Purpose: To provide member services and promote quality patient care for those suffering from sleep disorders.

**Association of Polysomno-graphic Technologists**
P.O. Box 14861
Lenexa, KS 66285
(913) 541-1991
Fax (913) 541-0156

**Association of Professional Sleep Societies**
1610 14th St. NW, Ste. 300
Rochester, MN 55901
(507) 287-6006
Fax (507) 287-6008
Purpose: An umbrella organization for professional organizations involved in sleep disorders: researchers, clinicians and clinical polysomnographers.

**ASAA A.W.A.K.E. Network (Alert, Well, And Keeping Energetic)**
P.O. Box 66
Belmont, MA 02178
(617) 489-4441
Fax (617) 489-4761
Purpose: A network of health awareness groups for patients with sleep apnea and sleep disordered breathing, with branches in most states.

**American Association of Sleep Services Providers**
Ambulatory Services of America
9 North Goodwin Avenue
Elmsford, NY 10528
(800) 540-4485
Fax (914) 277-7648
Purpose: A professional organization of individuals and businesses providing alternative-site sleep disorders diagnostic and therapeutic services.

**Better Sleep Council**
333 Commerce Street
Alexandria, VA 22314
(703) 683-8371
Fax (703) 683-4503
Purpose: To educate the general public about the importance of sleep in maintaining good health.

**Coalition to Wake Up America**
711 Second Street NE, Ste.200
Washington, D.C. 20002
(202) 544-7499
Purpose: An advocacy organization including professionals and citizens to support the work of the National Commission on Sleep Disorders.

**International Ventilator User's Network**
5100 Oakland Avenue, Ste.206
St. Louis, MO 63110
(314) 534-0475
Purpose: An organization linking ventilator users with each other and with appropriate health professionals.

**National Commission on Sleep Disorders Research**
Stanford University Sleep Disorders Center
701 Welch Road, Suite 2226
Palo Alto, CA 94304
(415) 725-6484
Fax (415) 725-7341
Purpose: A professional organization reporting to the National Institutes of Health, Congress, and the president on needs and priorities in sleep disorders research.

**National Foundation for Sleep and Related Disorders in Children**
4200 West Peterson Avenue, Suite 109
Chicago, IL 60646
(708) 368-6799
Purpose: To help and support parents; stimulate communication between researchers, physicians and patients; and to support research in sleep related disorders in children.

**National Institutes of Health**
National Center for Sleep Disorders Research
NHLB1, Building 31, Room 4A11
9000 Rockville Pike
Bethesda, MD 20892
(301) 496-4000
Purpose: To improve the health of the entire nation by expanding knowledge on sleep disorders.

**Narcolepsy Network**
P.O. Box 1365
FDR Station
New York, NY 10150
(914) 834-2855
Purpose: To address the needs of patients with narcolepsy and provide support services.

**National Sleep Foundation**
1367 Connecticut Avenue NW,
Suite 200
Washington, D.C. 20036
(202) 785-2300
Fax (202) 785-2880
Purpose: To improve the quality
of life for the billions of Americans who suffer from sleep
disorders and to prevent the
catastrophic accidents related to
poor or disordered sleep.

**Restless Legs Syndrome
Foundation**
1904 Banbury Road
Raleigh, NC 27608
(919) 571-1599
Fax (919) 571-9057
Purpose: To support patients
with restless legs syndrome and
their families.

**Sleep Disorders Dental
Society**
11676 Perry Highway,
Building 1, Suite 1204
Wexford, PA 15090
(412) 935-0836
Fax (412) 935-0383
Purpose: To improve treatment
for sleep related breathing disorders by dental practitioners.

**Sleep Research Society**
Laboratory for the Study of the
Brain in Sleep
University of Pennsylvania
Philadelphia, PA 19104-6045
(215) 898-8891
Fax (215) 573-2004
Purpose: To create new
knowledge about sleep disorders and to train future sleep
researchers.

# CANADA

**Canadian Sleep Society**
Camp Hill Medical Center,
Suite 4018
1763 Robie Street
Halifax
Nova Scotia B3H3G2
(902) 4964298

**Sleep/Wake Disorders
Canada**
3089 Bathurst Street, Suite 304
Toronto, Ontario M6A2A4
(416) 787-5374

# INTERNATIONAL

**Australasian Sleep Society**
Department of Respiratory
Medicine
Westmead Hospital
Westmead
New South Wales 2145
Australia

**Belgian Association for the
Study of Sleep**
Sleep/Wake Disorders Center
University Hospital of Antwerp
Wilrijkstraat 10
B-2650 Edegem
Belgium

**European Sleep Research
Society**
21 Rue Becquerel
Strasbourg 67087
France

**British Sleep Society**
P.O. Box 21
Lisburn
Coantrim  BT282SF
Northern Ireland

**British Snoring and Sleep Apnoea Association**
The Steps, How Lane
Chipstead
Surrey CR53LT
England

**Finnish Sleep Research Society**
Helsinki University Hospital
Dept. of Neurology
Haartmaninkatu 4
Fin-00290 Helsinki
Finland

**The Hong Kong Society of Sleep Medicine**
Haven of Hope Hospital
Po Lam Road South
Tseung Kwan O
Hong Kong

**The Insomnia and Snoring Cure Group**
Puncheston
Dyfed SA625RN
Wales

**Japanese Society of Sleep Research**
Department of Psychiatry
Kitasako University School
of Medicine
211 Asamizodai
Sagamihara
Kanagawa 228
Japan

**Latin American Sleep Society**
Depto. Biologica de la
Reproduccion
Universidad Autonoma
Metropolitana Iztapalapa
Av. Purisima y Michoacan
Apto. Postal 55535
Mexico City 09340
Mexico

**Netherlands Association for Sleep Apnea Patients**
DeNye Oanliz 25
9084 An Goutum
The Netherlands

**Sleep Group of the French Pneumology Society**
Hospital de Haute Pierre
Service Pneumologie
1 Ave. Moliere
Strasbourg 67098
France

**Sleep Society of South Africa**
P.O. Box 5331
Rivonia 2128
Republic of South Africa

**Swedish Sleep Disorder Association**
Neurofys Department
Södersjukhuset
5-11883 Stockholm
Sweden

# Product Manufacturers and Service Providers for Sleep-Related Breathing Disorders

## Monitoring & Diagnostic Equipment

**Ambulatory Monitoring Inc.**
731 Sawmill River Road
Ardsley, NY 10502-1608
(800) 341-0066
www.ambulatory-monitoring.com

**Atlanta School of Sleep
Medicine and Technology,
Northside Hospital Sleep
Disorders Center**
1000 Johnson Ferry Road, NE
Atlanta, GA 30342-1611
(800) 782-9418
www.sleepschool.com

**Bio-Logic Systems Corp.**
One Bio-Logic Plaza,
Mundeleim, IL 60060
(800) 323-8326
www.bio-logic.com

**Bionique**
34221 S. Wilhoit Road
Molalla, OR 97038
(503) 829-6520

**Cadwell Laboratories, Inc.**
909 N. Kellogg St.
Kennewick, WA 99336
(800) 245-3001
www.cadwell.com

**CNS Inc.**
1250 Park Road
Chanhassen, MN 55317
(612) 474-7600

**Datex-Ohmeda Inc.**
1315 W. Century Drive
Louisville, CO 80027
(800)345-2700
www.datex-ohmeda.com

**Discovery Software**
P.O. Box 531
Taylors, SC 29687
(800) 849-4410

**EdenTec**
10252 Valley View Road
Eden Prairie, MN 55344
(800) 826-2069

**Embla Medical Inc.**
555 N. Congress Avenue
Boynton Beach, FL 33426
(888)323-6252
www.emblamedical.com

**EPM Systems**
5212 Highberry Wood Rd.
Midlothian, VA 23112
(804) 739-7022

**ESC Medical Systems**
22011 30th Avenue SE
Bothell, WA 98021
(800) 548-1482

**Gereonics, Inc.**
4650-143 Dulin Road
Fallbrook, CA 92028
(619) 731-9003

**Grass Instrument Division**
600 E. Greenwich Avenue
West Warwick, RI 02893
(877) 472-4777
www.grassinstruments.com

**Hy-Tape Corp.**
772 McLean Avenue
Yonkers, NY 10704
(800) 248-0101
www.hytape.com

**IM Systems**
1045 Taylor Avenue, Suite 300
Baltimore, MD 21286
(410) 296-7723
www.imsystems.net

**Intercare Technologies, Inc.**
20875 Crossroads Circle, #300
Waukesha, WI 53186
(414) 798-2680

**Mallinckrodt Inc.**
675 McDonnell Blvd.
St. Louis, MO 63134
(800) 635-5267
www.mallinckrodt.com

**Martin Software and Consulting**
P.O. Box 36215
Hoover, AL 35236
(205) 733-1447

**Medcare**
401 Creekside Drive
Buffalo, NY 14228
(888) 662-7632
www.4medcare.com

**Melville Diagnostics**
1007-350 Sparks Street
Ottawa, Ontario K1R7S8
Canada
(613) 238-1291

**Midwest Sleep and Neurodiagnostic Institute**
6990 Meadow Song Trail
Rockford, IL 61109
(815) 873-8254

**Mini-Mitter Co., Inc.**
P.O. Box 3386
Sunriver, OR 97707
(800) 685-2999
www.minimitter.com

**Network Concepts**
2135 W. Greenview Drive
Middleton, WI 53562
(800) 877-1319

**Neurobase: Sleep Disorders, Arbor Publishing Co.**
4275 Executive Square, #305
San Diego, CA 92037-1476
(800) 452-2400

**Nicolet Instrument Corp.**
5225 Verona Road
Madison, WI 53711-4495
(800) 356-0007

**Nihon Kohden America**,
2601 Campus Drive
Irvine, CA 92715
(800) 325-0283

**Oxford Medical Inc.**
11526 53rd N. Street
Clearwater, FL 34616
(813) 573-4500

**Palco Labs**
8030 Soquel Avenue
Santa Cruz, CA 95062-2032
(800) 346-4488

**Radiometer America Inc.**
811 Sharon Drive
Westlake, OH 44145

**Rochester Electro-Medical Inc.**
15619 Premiere Dr., Ste. 204
Tampa, FL 33624
(800) 328-5544

**School of Sleep Medicine**
260 Sheridan Avenue
Palo Alto, CA 94306
(650) 326-1296
www.sleepedu.net

**Sensor Medics Corp.**
22705 Savi Ranch Parkway
Yorba Linda, CA 92687
(800) 231-2466

**Sleep Multimedia, Inc.**
P.O. Box 329-H
Scarsdale, NY 10583
(914) 722-9291

**Sleepline Aries Systems Corp.**
200 Sutton Street
N. Andover, MA 01845
(508) 975-7570

**SNAP Laboratory**
3633 West Lake Avenue, #406
Glenview, IL 60025
(800) 762-7786
www.snaplab.com

**Somnosoft, Inc.**
(888) 342-5781
www.somnosoft.com

**Stellate Systems**
345 Victoria Ave., Suite 300
Montreal, Quebec H3Z2N2
Canada
(888) 742-1306
www.stellate.com

**Synapse Media**
4702 Cloudcrest Drive
Medford, OR 97504
(541) 608-0381
www.synapsemedia.com

**Telediagnostic Systems**
2053 Sutter Street
San Francisco, CA 94115
(800) 227-3224

**Telefactor Corp.**
1094 New DeHaven Avenue
W. Conshohocken, PA 19428
(800) 425-3334

**The School of Clinical Polysomnography**
2268 Gene Cameron Way
Medford, OR 97504
(541) 857-1161
www.synapsemedia.com/school

**The School of Sleep Medicine**
2345 Yale Street
Palo Alto, CA 94306
(415) 493-0131

**Vitalog Respironics**
643 Bair Island Road
Suite 212
Redwood City, CA 94063
(415) 366-8676

# Treatment Devices and Equipment

**Airsep**
401 Creekside Drive
Buffalo, NY 14228
(888) 874-0202
www.airsep.com

**CPAP/PRO**
1515 Palisades Drive, Ste. M
Pacific Palisades, CA 90272
(800) 450-3566
www.cpappro.com

**DeVilbiss**
P.O. Box 635
Somerset, PA 15501
(814) 443-4881

**ENTec**
595 N. Pastoria Avenue
Sunnyvale, CA 94086
(800) 797-6520
www.entec.com

**ESC Medical Systems**
22011 30th Avenue SE
Bothell, WA 98021
(800) 548-1482

**External Nasal Dilator, CNS, Inc.**
1250 Park Road
Chanhassen, MN 55317-9260
(800) 843-2978

**Healthdyne Technologies**
1255 Kennestone Circle
Marietta, GA 30066
(800) 421-8754

**HGM Medical Laser Systems, Inc.**
3959 West 1820 South
Salt Lake City, UT 84104
(800) 447-0234

**Influence, Inc.**
71 Stevenson St., #1120
San Francisco, CA 94105
(888) 446-3583

**Innovative Medical Systems Inc.**
Lockheed Air Center
1050 Perimeter Road
Manchester, NH 03104
(800) 742-3646

**LifeCare**
655 Aspen Ridge Drive
Lafayette, CO 80026-9341
(303) 666-9234

**Lifesleep Systems, Inc.**
400 Oyster Point Blvd.
S. San Francisco, CA 94080
(877) Sleep-11/(877) 753-3711
www.lifesleep.com

**MedicAlert Foundation International**
2323 Colorado Ave.
Turlock, CA 95380
(800) 432-5378

**OPAP**
P.O. Box 189
Pioneer, CA 95666
(888) 590-9714
www.OPAP.com

**Puritan Bennett**
10800 Pfumm Road
Lenexa, KS 66215
(800) 248-0890

**ResCare, Inc.**
5744 Pacific Center Blvd.,#311
San Diego, CA 92121
(800) 424-0737

**ResMed Corp.**
10121 Carroll Canyon Road
San Diego, CA 92131
(800) 424-0737
www.resmed.com

Respironics, Inc.
1501 Ardmole Blvd.
Pittsburgh, PA 15221
(800) 345-6443
www.resmed.com

Snore Control, Sharper
Image Corp.
650 Davis Street
San Francisco, CA 94111
(800) 344-4444

Somnus
285 N. Wolfe Road
Sunnyvale, CA 94086
(888) 576-6687
www.somnus.com

Space Maintainers
Laboratory
9129 Lurline Avenue
Chatsworth, CA 91311
(800) 423-3270

Surgical Laser Technologies
200 Cresson Blvd.
Oaks, PA 19456-0880
(800) 366-4758

Surgilase, Inc.,
33 Plan Way
Warwick, RI 02886
(800) 537-5273

# Homecare Companies:
# Providers of CPAP

Abbey Home Health Care
33560 Hyland Ave.
Costa Mesa, CA 92626
(800) 777-2816

Ambulatory Services of
America
9 North Goodwin Avenue
Elmsford, NY 10523
(800) 540-4485

Amcare Medical Services,
Inc.
459 Watertown St.
Newton, MA 02160
(800) 669-1970

American Home Patient,
2414B Parkwood Dr.
Brunswick, GA 31520
(912) 264-5333

Homedco, Inc.
17650 New Hope St.
Fountain Valley, CA 92708
(800) 828-4894

Kimberley Quality Care
600 Century Plaza Dr., #165
Houston, TX 77073
(713) 821-7475

Lincare, Inc.
888 Executive Center Drive,
West, Suite 300
St. Petersburg, FL 33702
(800) 284-2006

National Medical Care, Inc.,
1601 Trapelow Road
Waltham, MA 02154
(800) 662-1237

Primedica
1841 W. Oak Parkway
West Oak Center
Marietta, GA 30062
(800) 647-3729

Protocare
950 Winter St.
Waltham, MA 02154
(617) 890-5560

# Appendix III

# A Guide to Medical Insurance for Sleep-Related Claims

## ICD-9 Coding

Every medical condition is identified by a coding method called the *International Classification of Diseases* (ICD), developed by the World Health Organization.

This ICD system, in which each condition is labeled by a 3-digit, 4-digit or 5-digit code, enables your medical insurance to accurately process any claim.

The system in current use is the 9th Revision, hence the term *ICD-9*. Here are the ICD-9 codes for some common sleep-related breathing disorders:

- Snoring                                        786.09
- Obstructive sleep apnea                         780.53
- Hypersomnolence (with sleep apnea)              780.53
- Chronic rhinitis                                472.0
- Chronic sinusitis                               473.0
- Nasal polyps                                    471.0
- Turbinate enlargement                           478.0
- Nasal septal deviation                          470.0
- Tonsillar enlargement                           474.1
- Adenoid enlargement                             474.12

# CPT Coding

Any surgical procedure or service rendered by a physician is identified by a 5-digit code. This system of *Current Procedural Terminology* (CPT) coding simplifies reporting to medical insurances, who can then accurately identify and reimburse any medical or surgical procedure/service. Here is a short list of representative CPT codes relevant to sleep-related breathing disorders:

## Procedure/Service

| | |
|---|---|
| ♦ Initial consultation | 99204 |
| ♦ Follow-up office visit | 99214 |
| ♦ Polysomnography | 95810 |
| ♦ Multiple sleep latency testing | 95805 |
| ♦ Laryngoscopy, fiberoptic | 31575 |
| ♦ Nasal CPAP therapy | 94660 |
| ♦ Uvulopalatopharyngoplasty | 42145 |
| ♦ Laser-assisted uvulopalatoplasty | 42145 |
| ♦ Tonsillectomy | 42826 |
| ♦ Adenoidectomy | 42830 |
| ♦ Nasal septoplasty | 30520 |
| ♦ Nasal turbinectomy | 30130 |

# Useful Terms Defined

**Acidosis:** Disturbance in acid-base balance; increased blood acidity.

**Adenoidectomy:** Surgical removal of the adenoids.

**Adenoids:** Spongy lymphoid tissue in the area behind the nose (nasopharynx).

**Apnea:** Cessation of breathing for 10 seconds or more.

**Apnea Index:** Calculation of the frequency of apnea.

**Arrhythmia:** Abnormal heart rhythm.

**Bradycardia:** Slowing of the heart rate.

**Carbon dioxide:** Waste gas removed from the blood stream in the lungs on exhaling.

**Cardiologist:** Physician specializing in the diagnosis and treatment of heart disease.

**Central sleep apnea:** Temporary cessation of breathing during sleep from failure of breathing effort.

**Circadian rhythm:** Biological rhythm of the alternating sleep-wake cycles in a 24-hour day.

**Coblation:** Technique for ablating or coagulating tissue.

**Collapsible airway:** Soft tissues in the upper respiratory tract lacking any rigid support.

**Computerized tomography:** Detailed multi-imaged x-ray.

**CPAP:** Continuous positive airway pressure; a device to treat obstructive sleep apnea.

**Deviated septum:** Deflection of the cartilage that creates the nasal partition, usually causing obstructed breathing.

**Diaphragm:** Muscular wall separating the chest cavity from the abdominal cavity, moving with respiration.

**D-sleep:** Phase of sleep in which we dream, synonymous with REM sleep.

**Electrocardiography (EKG):** Recording and measurement of electrical heart muscle activity.

**Electroencephalography (EEG):** Recording and measurement of brain waves.

**Electromyography (EMG):** Recording and measurement of electrical muscle activity.

**Electro-oculography (EOG):** Recording and measurement of eye-muscle movement.

**Enuresis:** Loss of bladder control, with bed-wetting during sleep.

**Hypercapnia:** Elevated blood level of carbon dioxide.

**Hypersomnolence:** Excessive tiredness or sleepiness during waking hours.

**Hypertension:** Elevated blood pressure.

**Hypopnea:** Reduced airflow (at least 50 percent) through the nose and mouth for 10 seconds or more.

**Hypotonia:** Reduced muscle tone.

**Hypoxemia:** Reduced blood level of oxygen.

**Impotence:** Inability to sustain penile erection.

**Insomnia:** Difficulty in getting to sleep and staying asleep.

**Laser:** Device producing concentrated light energy, used as a surgical tool to vaporize tissues.

**Laser-assisted uvulopalatoplasty (LAUP):** Surgery to shorten and reshape the uvula and soft palate.

**Mesopharyngometry:** Scientific method for measuring internal dimensions of the pharynx.

**Micro-arousal:** Brief awakening during sleep.

**Mixed sleep apnea:** Combination or coexistence of obstructive and central sleep apnea.

**Muscle tone:** Degree of muscle tension or relaxation.

**Myocardium:** Heart muscles.

**Narcolepsy:** Central nervous system condition causing excess drowsiness during waking hours.

**Nasal continuous positive airway pressure (Nasal CPAP):** Pump which generates a constant air pressure through the nose, used to treat sleep apnea.

**Nasal polyp:** Soft swelling arising from the mucous membrane of the nose or sinuses.

**Nasal polypectomy:** Surgical removal of polyps.

**Nasal septoplasty:** Surgery to correct a deviated nasal septum.

**Nasal septum:** Partition separating the two nasal cavities.

**Nasopharynx:** Area behind the nasal cavity, also referred to as the postnasal space.

**Neurologist:** Physician specializing in the diagnosis and treatment of nervous system disease.

**Nocturnal myoclonus:** Excess leg-muscle movement during sleep.

**Non-rapid eye movement sleep (NREM sleep):** Phase of sleep in which rapid eye movements do not occur.

**Obstructive sleep apnea:** Temporary cessation of breathing during sleep from obstruction in the upper airway.

**Otolaryngologist:** Physician specializing in the diagnosis and treatment of ear, nose and throat diseases.

**Oximeter:** Device to measure blood-oxygen saturation.

**Oxygen:** Gas essential for life. Carried to all tissues and organs by the red blood cells.

**Oxygen saturation:** Amount of oxygen carried in your blood. Used as a measure of sleep apnea.

**Palate:** Anatomic structure forming roof of the mouth.

**Parasomnias:** Various medical conditions that cause abnormal behavior during sleep.

**Polysomnogram:** Recording to measure a variety of physiological functions during sleep.

**Polysomnographer:** Physician or scientist trained in interpretation of data gathered by polysomnography.

**Pulmonologist:** Physician specializing in the diagnosis and treatment of lung diseases.

**Rapid eye movement sleep (REM sleep):** Phase of sleep denoted by rapid eye movements.

**Respiratory disturbance index:** Calculation of the frequency of apnea plus hypopnea.

**Sinuses:** Air-containing spaces closely related ot the nasal cavities.

**Sleep apnea:** Temporary cessation of breathing during sleep.

**Sleep cycles:** Stages of sleep denoted by changes in brain wave activity.

**Sleep disorders center (sometimes called sleep laboratory):** Diagnostic facility designed to study sleep-related medical conditions.

**Sleep fragmentation:** Interruption of the normal sleep cycle.

**Soft palate:** Soft part of palate, ending in the uvula.

**Somnoplasty:** Technique for reducing tissue volume utilizing radiofrequency electrical waves.

**Split-night study:** Single overnight sleep study for the purpose of recording sleep apnea and titrating nasal CPAP.

**Strain gauge:** Device for measuring expansion of the chest and abdomen during inspiration.

**Syndrome:** Group of related symptoms, for example, the sleep apnea syndrome.

**Tachycardia:** Increase in heart rate.

**Thermistor:** Temperature-sensitive device to record airflow through the nose and mouth.

**Tonsil:** Spongy lymphoid tissue mass on either side of the pharynx.

**Tonsillectomy:** Surgical removal of the tonsils.

**Tracheostomy:** Surgery to open the windpipe.

**Turbinate:** Bony structure on side wall of the nose.

**Turbinectomy:** Surgery to reduce the tissues on the inside walls of the nose.

**Upper airway resistance syndrome:** Medical condition characterized by severe snoring and daytime sleepiness.

**Upper respiratory tract:** Air passages leading to the lungs, structures included here are the nose, sinuses, throat and larynx.

**Uvula:** Tongue-like structure attached to soft palate.

**Uvulopalatopharyngoplasty (UPPP):** Surgery to enlarge the air passages in the back of the throat.

**Vasomotor rhinitis:** Condition produced by an imbalance in nasal blood circulation, resulting in chronic nasal congestion.

# Bibliography

## Popular Magazine Articles on Snoring

"How Can George Stop Snoring!" *Ladies' Home Journal*, April, 1915, 32:54.

"Why We Snore." *Literary Digest*, 1924, 82:27.

Bilik, S. "About Why People Snore." *Hygeia*, 1946, 24:820.

Dugan, James. "Bedlam in the Boudoir" *Collier's*, 1947, 119:17.

"For Sonorous Sleepers." *Newsweek*, 1949, 33:46.

"Conquest of Snoring Claimed." *Science*, 1950, 58:359.

"A Cure for Snoring." *Scientific American*, 1951, 184:35.

"A Cure for Snoring." *Today's Health*, April, 1953, 31:6.

"Husband's Snore Claimed Sign of Affection." *Science Digest*, 1954, 35:29.

Fabricant, Noah. "Sound Facts About Snoring." *Today's Health*, 1958, 36:18.

Waggoner, Walter. "About Snoring." *New York Times Magazine*, Oct., 1960, 16:43.

"Can Snoring Be Cured?" *Good Housekeeping*, 1962, 155:137.

Van Buren, Abigail. "Is There a Snorer in the House?" *Reader's Digest*, 1966, 89:114.

Snider, A. "Putting a Stop to Snoring." *Science Digest*, 1972, 71:59.

"Help for Snorers." *Modern Maturity*, 1976, 19:15.

Cohen, Marcia. "Things That Go Z-Z-Z in the Night." *Ladies' Home Journal*, 1976, 93:56.

Buffington, P. "The Sounds of Sleep." *Saturday Evening Post*, 1981, 253:74.

"How to Get a Good Night's Sleep With a Man." *Glamour*, 1981, 79:146.

"Snore-Breakers." *Fifty Plus*, 1981, 21:26.

"Snoring Cure." *Omni*, 1981, 4:49.

"The Better Mouth Trap." *Weightwatchers*, 1982, 15:12.

251

Cox, James. "Snorers! Don't Despair! There Will Always be UPPP." *Smithsonian*, 1983, 14:174.

"A Snip for A Snorer." *Health*, 1983, 15:22.

Kiester, E. "A Little Night Music." *Fifty Plus*, 1984, 24:68.

Lustig, Bill. "How to Be A Better Bedmate." *Glamour*, 1984, 82:56.

"New Surgical Treatment for Snoring." *USA Today*, 1984, 112:11.

Pechter, Kerry. "Surprising Facts About Snoring and Health." *Prevention*, 1984, 36:26.

"Relief for Nocturnal Noisemakers." *Science*, 1984, 5:92.

"Snore Wars: Surgery for Snorers." *Reader's Digest*, 1984, 124:26.

"Snoring." *Good Housekeeping*, 1984, 199:58.

Wasco, James M.D. "All About Snoring from A to Z-Z-Z's." *Woman's Day*, 1984, September 9.

"Can You Snooze If He Snores?" *Mademoiselle*, 1985, 91:50.

"Snoring and Angina: A Link?" *Prevention*, 1985, 37:7.

"Snoring, Not Just An Annoying Habit, But A Call for Help." *Better Homes and Gardens* 1985, 63:72.

Savaiano, Jacqueline. "The Plight of the Thunderous Snorer." *People*, 1986, November 17.

Mitchell, Cynthia F. "Firms Waking Up to Sleep Disorders." *Wall Street Journal*, 1988, July 7.

"Nine Bed-tested Snore Stoppers." *Prevention*, 1989, March.

Rolbein, Seth. "Bizarre Sleep Disorders." *Good Housekeeping*, 1989, May.

Lipman, M.D. Derek S. "Snoring, Nuisance of the Night." *Compass Readings*, 1990, October.

"Five Ways to Better Sleep." *Men's Health*, 1991, August.

"The ZZZZZZ Plan." *Prevention*, 1992, January.

Kramer, Louise. "Prisoner of Sleep." *Redbook*, 1993, January.

# Suggested Books on Sleep and its Disorders

Borbely, A.A. *Secrets of Sleep*. New York: Basic Books, 1986.

Boulware, Marcus H. *Snoring*. New Jersey: American Faculty Press, 1974.

Cartwright, Rosalind. *A Primer on Sleep and Dreaming*. Reading, MA: Addison-Wesley Publishing Company, 1978.

Cartwright, Rosalind. *Night Life: Explorations in Dreaming*. New Jersey: Prentice-Hall, 1977.

Catalano, Ellen Mohr. *Getting to Sleep*. California: New Harbinger Publications, 1990.

Dement, William. *Some Must Watch While Some Must Sleep*. New York: Charles Scribner and Sons, 1972.

Fairbanks, David N.F., Shiro Fujita, and Takenosuke Ikematsu. *Snoring and Obstructive Sleep Apnea*. New York: Raven Press, 1994.

Freud, Sigmund. *On Dreams*. New York: N.W. Norton, 1952.

Freud, Sigmund. *The Interpretation of Dreams*. London: Allen and Unwin, 1954.

Fritz, Roger. *Sleep Disorders: America's hidden nightmare*. Illinois: National Sleep Alert, 1993.

Guilleminault, Christian. *Sleep and Its Disorders in Children*. New York: Raven Press, 1987.

Guilleminault, Christian and William Dement. *Sleep Apnea Syndromes*. New York: Alan R. Liss, 1978.

Hales, Dianne. *The Complete Book of Sleep*. Massachusetts: Addison-Wesley, 1981.

Hauri, Peter J., and Shirley Linde. *No More Sleepless Nights*. New York: John Wiley and Sons, 1990.

Hirsch, S.C. *Theater of the night. What We Do and Do Not Know About Dreams*. Chicago: Rand McNally, 1976.

Hobson, J. Allan. *The Dreaming Brain*. New York: Basic Books, 1988.

Hoskisson, J.B. *What is This Thing Called Sleep?* London: David-Poynter, 1976.

Johnson, T. Scott, and Jerry Halberstadt. *Phantom of the Night*. Cambridge: New Technology Publishing, 1995.

Kleitman, Nathaniel. *Sleep and Wakefulness*. Chicago: University of Chicago Press, 1963.

Kryger, Meir H., Thomas Roth and William Dement. *Principles and practice of Sleep Medicine.* Second Edition. Philadelphia: W.B. Saunders, 1994.

Lamberg, Lynne. *The American Medical Association Guide to Better Sleep.* New York: Random House, 1984.

Linde, Shirley, and Louis M. Savary. *The Sleep Book.* New York: Harper and Rowe, 1974.

Mendelson, Wallace. *Human Sleep and Its Disorders.* New York: Plenum Press, 1977.

Moore-Ede, M., F. Sulzman, and C. Fuller. *The Clocks That Time Us.* Massachusetts: Harvard University Press, 1982.

Orr, William C., Kenneth Altshuler and Monte Stahl. *Managing Sleep Complaints.* Chicago:Yearbook Medical Publishers, 1982.

Parkes, J.D. *Sleep and Its Disorders.* Philadelphia: W.B. Saunders, 1985.

Riley, Terrence. *Clinical Aspects of Sleep and Sleep Disturbance.* New York: Butterworths, 1985.

Rosenthal, Lois. *How To Stop Snoring.* Cincinnati: Writer's Digest Books, 1986.

Saunders, Nicholas A. and Colin E. Sullivan. *Sleep and Breathing.* New York: Marcel Dekker, 1993.

Thorpy, Michael J. *Handbook of Sleep Disorders.* New York: Marcel Dekker, 1990.

Williams, Robert L. *Sleep Disorders: Diagnosis and Treatment.* New York: Wiley, 1978.

# Selected Papers from the Medical Literature

American Sleep Disorders Association Report. "Practice Parameters for the Use of Laser-Assisted Uvulopalatoplasty." *Sleep,* 1994; 17:744.

American Sleep Disorders Association Report. "Portable Recording in the Assessment of Obstructive Sleep Apnea." *Sleep,* 1994; 17:378.

Bailey, B.J. "Problematic Snoring and Sleep Apnea: The Place for Surgery." *Archives of Otolaryngology,* 1984; 110:491.

Becker, K., and J. Cummiskey. "Managing Sleep Apnea: What are Today's Options?" *The Journal of Respiratory Diseases,* June 1985. 50

Berry, R.B., and A.J. Block. "Positive Nasal Airway Pressure Eliminates Snoring As Well As Obstructive Sleep Apnea." *Chest,* 1984; 85:15.

Block, A.J. "Is Snoring A Risk Factor?" *Chest.* 2981; 80:525.

Bradley, T.G., and E.A. Phillipson. "Pathogenesis and Pathophysiology of the Obstructive Sleep Apnea Syndrome." *Medical Clinics of North America,* 1985; 69:1169.

Bradley, T.G., and E.A. Phillipson. "Central Sleep Apnea." *Clinics in Chest Medicine,* 1992; 13:493.

Broomes, E.L. "New Thoughts On Snoring Prevention." *Journal of the National Medical Association,* 1982; 74:1139.

Browman, C.P., et al. "Hypersomnia: Diagnosis and Management." *Comprehensive Therapy,* 1983; 9:67.

Champion, P.C. "The Management of Snoring." *Medical Journal of Australia,* 1985; 143:337.

Chervin, R.D., et al. "Symptoms of Sleep Disorders, Inattention and Hyperactivity in Children." *Sleep,* 1997; 20:1185.

Conway, W., et al. "Uvulopalatopharyngoplasty: One Year Follow-Up." *Chest,* 1988; 88:345.

Dayal, V.S. and E.A. Phillipson. "Nasal Surgery in the Management of Sleep Apnea." *Annals of Otorhinolaryngology,* 1985; 94:550.

Downey, R., R.M. Perkin, and J. MacQuarrie. "Upper Airway Resistance Syndrome: Sick, Symptomatic but Under Recognized." *Sleep,* 1993; 16:620.

Engleman, H.M., S.E. Martin, and N.J. Douglas. "Compliance With CPAP Therapy in Patients With Sleep Apnea/Hypop-nea Syndrome." *Thorax,* 1994; 49:263.

Fairbanks, D.N. "Effects of Nasal Surgery on Snoring." *Southern Medical Journal,* 1985; 78:268.

Fairbanks, D.N. "Snoring: Surgical vs. Nonsurgical Treatment." *Laryngoscope,* 1984; 94:1188.

Felstein, I. "Snoring: The Sufferer Who Doesn't Suffer." *Nursing Mirror,* 1979; 148:42.

Fujita, S. "Uvulopalatopharyngoplasty For Sleep Apnea and Snoring." *Ear, Nose and Throat Journal,* 1984; 63:227.

Fujita, S., et al. "Evaluation of the Effectiveness of Uvulopalato-pharyngoplasty." *Laryngoscope,* 1985; 95:70.

Ghoneim, M.D. "Mechanism of Snoring." *Journal of the American Medical Association,* 1981; 245:1729.

Gislason, T., et al. "Prevalence of Sleep Apnea Syndrome Among Swedish Men: An Epidemiological Study." *Journal of Clinical Epidemiology,* 1988; 41:571.

Gluckman, J.L. "The Clinical Approach to Nasal Obstruction." *The Journal of Respiratory Diseases,* April, 1983;13.

Goldstein, J.A. "Possible Therapy For Snoring." *Western Medical Journal,* 1983; 138:270.

Goldstein, J.A. "Protriptyline For Snoring." *New England Medical Journal,* 1983; 308:1602.

Gozal, D. "Sleep Disordered Breathing and School Performance in Children." *Pediatrics,* 1998; 102:616.

Guilleminault, C., et al. "Sleep Apnea in Eight Children." *Pediatrics,* 1976; 58:23.

Guilleminault, C., et al. "A Cause of Excessive Daytime Sleepiness: The Upper Airway Resistance Syndrome." *Chest,* 1993; 104:781.

Guilleminault, C., R. Stoohs and S. Duncan. "Snoring: Daytime Sleepiness in Regular Heavy Snorers." *Chest,* 1991; 99:40.

Guilleminault, C. "Obstructive Sleep Apnea: The Clinical Syndrome and Historical Perspective." *Medical Clinics of North America,* 1985; 69:1187.

Haraldsson, P.O., et al. "Long-Term Effect of Uvulopalatophar-yngoplasty on Driving Performance." *Archives of Otolaryngology,* 1995; 121:90.

Haraldsson, P.O., and C. Carenfelt. "Laser Uvulopalatoplasty in Local Anesthesia. A Safe Approach in the Treatment of Habitual Snoring." *Rhinology,* 1990; 28:65.

Hausfeld, J.N. "Fiberoptic Manipulation of the Upper Airway and the Preoperative Assessment for Uvulopalatopharyngo-plasty." *Laryngoscope,* 1985; 95:738.

Issa, F.G., and C.E. Sullivan. "Alcohol, Snoring and Sleep Apnea." *Journal of Neurology, Neurosurgery and Psychiatry,* 1982; 45:353.

Jennett, S. "Snoring and Its Treatment." *British Medical Journal,* 1984; 289:335.

Johns, M.W. "A New Method for Measuring Daytime Sleepiness: The Epworth Sleepiness Scale." *Sleep*, 1991; 14:540.

Kamami, Y.V. "Laser $CO_2$ For Snoring: Preliminary Results. *Acta Otorhinolaryngologica*, 1990; 44:451.

Kamami, Y.V. "Outpatient Treatment of Sleep Apnea Syndrome With $CO_2$ Laser." *Journal of Clinical Laser Medicine and Surgery*, 1994; 12:215.

Katsantonis, G.P., et al. "The Surgical Treatment of Snoring: A Patient's Perspective." *Laryngoscope*, 1990; 100:138.

Keenan, S.P., et al. "Long-Term Survival of Patients with Obstructive Sleep Apnea Treated by Uvulopalatopharyngoplasty or Nasal CPAP." *Chest*, 1994; 105:155.

Koskenvuo, M., et al. "Snoring As A Risk Factor For Ischeaemic Heart Disease and Stroke in Men." *British Medical Journal*, 1987; 294:16.

Krespi, Y.P., et al. "The Efficacy of Laser-Assisted Uvulopalatoplasty in the Management of Obstructive Sleep Apnea and Upper Airway Resistance Syndrome. *Operative Techniques in Otolaryngology-Head and Neck Surgery*, 1995; 5:235.

Krespi, Y.P. and A. Keidar. "Laser-Assisted Uvulopalatoplasty for the Treatment of Snoring." *Operative Techniques in Otolaryngology-Head and Neck Surgery*, 1994; 5:228.

Loughlin, G.N. "Obstructive Sleep Apnea in Older Children." *The Journal of Respiratory Diseases*, Oct., 1982; 10.

MacNab, T., A. Blokmanis, and R.I. Dickson. "Long-Term Results of Uvulopalatopharyngoplasty for Snoring." *Otolaryngology*, 1992; 21:350.

Morton, R.P., et al. "Surgery for Snoring—What Constitutes A Cure?" *New Zealand Medical Journal*, 1985; 98:352.

Norton, P.E., E.V. Dunn, and J.S. Height. "Snoring in Adults: Some Epidemiologic Aspects." *Canadian Medical Association Journal*, 1983; 128:674.

Pelausa, E.O. and L.M. Tarshis. "Surgery For Snoring." *Laryngoscope*, 1989; 99:1006.

Powell, N., et al. "Obstructive Sleep Apnea, Continuous Positive Airway Pressure and Surgery." *Otolaryngology—Head and Neck Surgery*, 1988; 99:362.

Powell, N., et al. "Radiofrequency Volumetric Tissue Reduction for Treatment of Turbinate Hypertrophy: a Pilot Study." *Otolaryngology—Head and Neck Surgery*, 1999; 119:569.

Powell, N., et al. "Radiofrequency Tongue Base Reduction in Sleep-Disordered Breathing: a Pilot Study." *Otolaryngology—Head and Neck Surgery,* 1996; 120:656.

Powell, N., et al. "Radiofrequency Volumetric Tissye Reduction of the Palate in Subjects with Sleep-Disordered Breathing." *Otolaryngology—Head and Neck Surgery,* 1998; 113:1163.

Reeves-Hochen, K., R. Meck and C.W. Zwillich. "Nasal CPAP: An Objective Evaluation of Patient Compliance." *American Journal of Respiratory and Critical Care Medicine,* 1994; 149:149.

Rice, D.H. and M. Persky. "Snoring: Clinical Implications and Treatment." *Otolaryngology-Head and Neck Surgery,* 1986; 95:28.

Rice, D.H. "Snoring and Obstructive Sleep Apnea." *Medical Clinics of North America,* 1991; 75:1367.

Riley, R.W., N. Powell, and C. Guilleminault. "Current Concepts for Treating Obstructive Sleep Apnea." *Journal of Maxillofacial Surgery,* 1987; 45:149.

Riley, R.W., et al. "Obstructive Sleep Apnea: Trends in Therapy." *The Western Journal of Medicine,* 1995; 162:143.

Rolfe, I., L.G. Olson and N.A. Saunders. "Long-Term Acceptance of continuous Positive Airway Pressure in Obstructive Sleep Apnea." *American Review of Respiratory Disease,* 1991; 144:1130.

Saunders, N.A., et al. "Uvulopalatopharyngoplasty as a treatment for Snoring." *Medical Journal of Australia,* 1989; 150:177.

Sher, A.E. "Obstructive Sleep Apnea Syndrome: A Complex Disorder of the Upper Airway." *The Otolaryngologic Clinics of North America,* 1990; 23:593.

Sher, A.E. "The Efficacy of Surgical Modifications of the Upper Airway in Adults with Obstructive Sleep Apnea Syndrome." *Sleep,* 1996; 19:156.

Simmons, F.B., et al. "Snoring and Some Obstructive Sleep Apnea Can Be Cured by Oropharyngeal Surgery." *Archives of Otolaryngology,* 1983; 109:503.

Simmons, F.B., et al. "A Surgical Treatment for Snoring and Obstructive Sleep Apnea." *Western Journal of Medicine,* 1984; 140:43.

Smolley, L.A. "Obstructive Sleep Apnea: Avoiding Diagnostic Pitfalls." *The Journal of Respiratory Diseases,* 1990; 6:547.

Songshan, Z. "Successful Treatment of Sleep Apnea Syndrome by Transfusion of Vital Energy." *Chinese Medical Journal,* 1980; 93:279.

Stradling, J.R. and E.A. Phillipson. "Breathing Disorders During Sleep." *Quarterly Journal of Medicine,* 1986; 225:3.

Strohl, K.P., B. Cherniack, and B. Gothe. "Physiologic Basis of Therapy for Sleep Apnea." *American Review of Respiratory Diseases,* 1986; 134:791.

Sullivan, C.E., and F.G. Issa, "Pathophysiological Mechanisms in Obstructive Sleep Apnea." *Sleep,* 1980; 314:235.

Sussman, D., et al. "The Pickwickian Syndrome With Hypertrophy of Tonsils." *Laryngoscope,* 1975; 85:565.

Taasan, V.C., et al. "Alcohol Increases Sleep Apnea and Oxygen Desaturation in Asymptomatic Men. *The American Journal of Medicine,* 1981; 71:240.

Tirlapur, V.G. "Snoring as a Risk Factor for Hypertension and Angina." *Lancet,* 1985; 1:1340.

Walker, R.P., et al. "Laser-Assisted Uvulopalatoplasty for Snoring and Obstructive Sleep Apnea: Results in 170 Patients." *Laryngoscope,* 1995; 105:938.

Walker, R.P., et al. "Uvulopalatopharyngoplasty Versus Laser-Assisted Uvulopalatoplasty for the Treatment of Obstructive Sleep Apnea." *Laryngoscope,* 1997; 107:76.

Wennmo, C., et al. "Treatment of Snoring: With and Without Carbon Dioxide Laser." *Acta Otolaryngologica,* 1992;92:152.

Westbrook, P.R. "The Chronically Snoring Child: An Acoustic Annoyance or Cause for Concern?" *Mayo Clinical Proceedings,* 1983; 58:399.

Wilson, K., et al. "Snoring: An Acoustic Monitoring Technique." *Laryngoscope,* 1985; 95:1174.

Woolford, T., and T. Farrington. "Laser-Assisted Uvulopalatoplasty: The British Method." *Operative Techniques in Otolaryngology-Head and Neck Surgery,* 1994; 5:292.

Yamashiro, Y. and M.H. Kryger. "CPAP Titration For Sleep Apnea Using a Split-Night Protocol." *Chest,* 1995; 107:62.

Zwillich, C. "The Clinical Significance of Snoring." *Archives of Internal Medicine,* 1979; 139:24.

# Index

# Yes! I know a snorer/snoree who needs help. . .

For more information, visit our web site:

**www.drlipmansnoring.com**

## A Note on the Type

The text of this book was set in ITC Galliard, a typeface adapted by Matthew Carter from the sixteenth-century designs of Robert Granjon and introduced by the Mergenthaler Linotype Company in 1978. The designer has captured the vitality of the early forms, producing a contemporary rendition at once distinctive, elegant and extremely readable.

*Cover design:* Chris Pearl
*Illustrations:* Geoffrey Sauncy and
Joan Livermore, C.M.I.
*Text Design:* Mary Jo Zazueta
*Production Editor:* Gladys Haldanish
*Editorial Assistants:* Sarah Bellum, Christa Galli,
Buck Sinator, Natalie d'Rest
*Printing and Binding:* Sheridan Books, Inc.,
Chelsea, Michigan